POVERTY AND THE TRANSITION TO A MARKET ECONOMY IN MONGOLIA

Poverty and the Transition to a Market Economy in Mongolia

Edited by

Keith Griffin
Professor of Economics
University of California, Riverside

St. Martin's Press

First published in Great Britain 1995 by
MACMILLAN PRESS LTD
Houndmills, Basingstoke, Hampshire RG21 2XS
and London
Companies and representatives
throughout the world

A catalogue record for this book is available
from the British Library.

ISBN 0–333–63741–0

10   9   8   7   6   5   4   3   2   1
04   03   02   01   00   99   98   97   96   95

Printed and bound in Great Britain by
Antony Rowe Ltd
Chippenham, Wiltshire

First published in the United States of America 1995 by
Scholarly and Reference Division,
ST. MARTIN'S PRESS, INC.,
175 Fifth Avenue,
New York, N.Y. 10010

ISBN 0–312–12577–1 (cloth)

Library of Congress Cataloging-in-Publication Data
Poverty and the transition to a market economy in Mongolia / edited by
Keith Griffin.
p. cm.
Includes bibliographical references and index.
ISBN 0–312–12577–1 (cloth)
1. Mongolia—Economic policy.   2. Mixed economy—Mongolia.
3. Mongolia—Economic conditions.   4. Poverty—Mongolia.
I. Griffin, Keith B.
HC430.25.P68 1995
338.951'7—dc20   94–46184
                                                        CIP

Contents

Preface

Mongolia is a large country in north-central Asia, larger than the UK, France, Germany and Italy combined. It occupies the area from the Gobi desert to southern Siberia that separates China from Russia. It is a country of deserts and steppes and long, harsh winters. Not many people live on this land: the population is only two-and-a-quarter million and the population density, at 1.4 persons per square kilometre, is one of the lowest in the world. Mongolia is historically a land of nomads, and just over half of the population today lives in urban areas. Nomadic livestock continues to dominate the economy and about a quarter of all households continue to follow a nomadic way of life. Sixty per cent of the population, including many who live in the cities, dwell in herders' tents or *gers*.

For six-and-a-half decades, between 1924 and 1989, Mongolia was a communist country. There was a single party, the Mongolian People's Revolutionary Party, which had a monopoly of political power. Economic power was equally concentrated either in state-owned enterprises or in livestock cooperatives (*negdels*) and resources were allocated not by the market but in accordance with a system of central planning. All of this changed suddenly in 1989: the Russians left, multi-party elections were held and the country embarked on a transition from a centrally planned to a market-guided economy.

Alas, the transition in Mongolia has not gone smoothly. If one compares 1989 (the year before the transition began) with 1993 (the last year for which data are available) it appears that many indicators point to a decline in well-being and a rise in distress. Average incomes declined by about 30 per cent. Unemployment, virtually unknown before the transition, rose dramatically. Those officially designated as living in poverty rose from virtually none to 27 per cent of the population by March 1994. The decline in material well-being was accompanied by a deterioration in health status. The number of people recorded as suffering from mental disorders – mostly depression – rose sharply; the morbidity rate increased by more than 80 per cent; the maternal mortality rate also appears to have risen. The difficulties of the transition are reflected, too, in indicators of social disorder and stress. The number of reported crimes, for instance, increased by 166 per cent between 1990 and 1993. Politically, Mongolia has remained stable and nonviolent, but strains in the polity are beginning to appear and the hunger strike in the central square of the capital city, Ulaanbaatar, in April 1994 is perhaps an early warning that the population may be running out of patience.

One of the most striking responses to the decline in well-being and the rise in poverty was a decline in the birth rate. During the era of central planning, Mongolia had pursued a pro-natalist policy and although birth rates had been falling gradually they were still 36.4 per thousand in 1989. The hardship that accompanied the transition to a market economy, however, led women to choose to have fewer children and as a result, by 1993 the birth rate had fallen to 21.5 per thousand. That is, the birth rate fell by nearly 41 per cent in just four years. Had the birth rate and the population growth rate remained at previous levels the rise in poverty undoubtedly would have been even more alarming. In fact, however, the population growth rate was cut in half, falling from 2.8 per cent a year in 1989 to 1.4 per cent in 1993 and this helped to mitigate the deterioration in the country's standard of living.

Changes in the nine indicators of well-being to which I have referred are presented in Table 1. Many of them are discussed more fully in the chapters that follow.

The transition to a market economy not only was *accompanied* by a fall in average incomes, a rise in income inequality and a huge increase in poverty, but the economic policies intended to effect the transition were the primary *cause* of the decline in well-being. The deterioration in living conditions, in turn, led the government to give high priority to the alleviation and ultimately the elimination of poverty. The United Nations Development Programme (UNDP) was asked by the government to assist in preparing an assessment of the poverty situation in the country and to help in preparing a concrete programme of action that could be implemented with a minimum of delay. The UNDP, in turn, organised a mission, assigned it the task of preparing an analytical assessment and making policy recommendations, and asked me to lead it. This volume began life as the report of that mission.

The research team consisted of Keith Griffin (University of California, Riverside), Seamus Cleary (consultant), Nadia Forni (United Nations Food and Agriculture Organisation), Wouter van Ginneken (International Labour Organisation), Joyce Lannert (consultant), Barbara Skapa (consultant), Sheila Smith (UNDP) and Jeremy Swift (Institute of Development Studies, University of Sussex). Administrative services in Ulaanbaatar were provided by Geraldine Picar (on secondment from UNDP, Pyongyang),

TABLE 1 Indicators of declining well-being in Mongolia, 1989–93
(index: 1989 = 100 except where otherwise indicated)

	GNP per capita	Registered unemployment	Mental disorders	Crime rate	Poverty incidence (%)	Morbidity rate	Maternal mortality rates (per 10K live births)	Crude birth rate (per thousand)	Population growth rate (%)
1989	100	100	100*	n.a.	0	100*	13	36.4	2.8
1990	95	152	139	100	n.a.	121	12	35.3	2.7
1991	84	185	382	148	n.a.	184	13	32.9	2.4
1992	78	180	358	171	17	172	20	29.1	2.1
1993	70	240	n.a.	266	24**	n.a.	n.a.	21.5	1.4

* 1985
** 27% in March 1994

Gillian Pereira (on secondment from UNDP, Beijing) and Jadamba Oyuntuya (UNDP, Ulaanbaatar). Michael Reynolds (UNDP, Ulaanbaatar) assisted us as a liaison officer. Kathy Lowney prepared the manuscript for publication in Riverside, California.

I made three trips to Mongolia in spring and early summer of 1994. The research team had access to the published literature relevant to poverty issues as well as to large numbers of government documents and unpublished reports prepared by multilateral and bilateral agencies and non-governmental organisations. We had numerous helpful discussions with government officials, members of national and international non-governmental organisations, and officials of international and bilateral agencies. Field trips were conducted to five *aimags* (provinces), namely, Dornod, Ovorkhangai, South Gobi, Tov and Zavhan.

This book should be of interest, I believe, to three groups of readers. First, I hope it will be thought provoking and useful to those concerned with Mongolia and East Asia in general, including those responsible for recommending or formulating policies in the region. Second, the book can be seen as a contribution to the widespread debate on the economic transition from centrally-planned to market-guided economies, a debate that includes the former USSR, Eastern and Central Europe, China, North Korea, Vietnam and possibly Cuba. Third, the book should be of use to those interested in human development strategies and the alleviation of poverty in developing countries. In fact this volume can be read as an attempt to apply in a specific country some of the more general ideas developed in a recent book by Terry McKinley and myself, *Implementing a Human Development Strategy*. I am very grateful to the United Nations Resident Representative in Mongolia, Jan Swietering, for his encouragement and support. He and his very able staff did everything possible to ensure that the work of the team proceeded smoothly. Without the assistance of the UNDP staff it would not have been possible to complete such a large study in such a short period of time. Jan Swietering saw from the beginning the importance of the study and the need to ensure its wide dissemination.

My greatest gratitude, however, is to our Mongolian colleagues. I appreciate the confidence expressed in the research team by offering us a delicate and difficult assignment. I appreciate the honesty and candour of everyone with whom we came in contact, and the willingness of government officials to discuss serious problems openly and to show us firsthand the evidence of poverty we had come to study. Our official host in Mongolia was the Ministry of Population Policy and Labour. I am grateful to its Minister, Mr Erdene Gombojav, for facilitating our work, opening doors for us and expressing a keen interest in our conclusions. I am also grateful to the members of the National Council of Poverty Alleviation and to the members of the coordinating group and four working groups of the Council for the interest they took in our studies and the assistance they gave us. Lastly, I would like to give special thanks to Ms Harloo Enkhjargal, the Director-General of the Population and Social Policy Department of the Ministry of Population Policy and Labour and head of the secretariat of the National Council. Mrs Enkhjargal devoted an extraordinary amount of time to ensuring the success of our work and we are very grateful to her.

The views expressed in this volume are, of course, those of the authors; they do not necessarily reflect the views of UNDP or of the government of Mongolia.

KEITH GRIFFIN

Notes on the Contributors

Seamus Cleary is a development consultant, specialising in participatory methods of identification, monitoring and evaluation of development projects and the activities of the international financial institutions. His clients include academic institutions, multilateral development organisations and NGOs. Before establishing his consultancy business in 1991, he was senior Policy Researcher at the London-based Catholic Fund for Overseas Development and president of the Policy Advisory Group of the 14-member Brussels-based international Catholic development NGO network, Cooperation internationale pour le developpement et la solidarité (Cidse).

Nadia Forni is an Italian national with an academic background in political science and agricultural economics. She is a Senior Officer for employment and manpower planning in the Human Resources, Institutions and Agrarian Reform Division of the Food and Agriculture Organisation of the United Nations. She is particularly concerned with the employment aspects of pastoral development and with the transformation of command to market-oriented economies.

Keith Griffin is Professor of Economics of the University of California, Riverside. He was formerly President of Magdalen College, Oxford. He has served as an adviser and consultant to various governments, international agencies and academic institutions in Asia, Africa and Latin America. He is the author of *Alternative Strategies for Economic Development*, co-author of *Implementing a Human Development Strategy* and co-editor of *The Distribution of Income in China*, among other books.

Joyce M. Lannert has an MA in Public Administration from New York University and is a Member of the American Institute of Certified Planners (AICP). She has worked as a housing specialist in the United States and on various development programmes in Egypt, Jordan, Lebanon, the United Arab Emirates and China. She is currently a development consultant based in the United States.

Barbara C. Skapa is a development consultant who has specialised

xiii

in promoting small and medium-scale businesses and associated services such as credit and technical assistance. She has considerable experience with employment creation projects designed to encourage gender equity. When not engaged in consulting, Ms Skapa can be found in Mt Vernon, Maine where she operates a seasonal mushroom export business.

Sheila Smith is currently Senior Economist in the Policy Division of UNDP in New York. She has taught economics at the Universities of Liverpool, Cambridge and Sussex. Her publications include *Poverty, Class and Gender in Rural Africa: A Tanzanian Case Study* (with John Sender), *The Development of Capitalism in Africa* (with John Sender), and *Trade and Poor Economies* (edited with John Toye). She holds an MSc from the University of Guelph and a PhD from the University of Manchester.

Jeremy Swift has a DPhil in Development Economics from the University of Sussex and is a Fellow of the Institute of Development Studies at the University of Sussex. He specialises in arid land and mountain environments and especially pastoral economies. Recent work has included work on pastoral land tenure and development institutions, liberalisation of the centrally planned pastoral economies of Central Asia, the theory and history of famine, and policies and practice in food security. He has worked extensively in West and East Africa, the Middle East and Central Asia. From 1989 he has coordinated a large interdisciplinary research project on the liberalisation of the pastoral economy of Mongolia.

Wouter van Ginneken is a development economist and staff member of the International Labour Office. He is currently Senior Policy Analyst of the Social Security Department. He has published on income distribution, employment and social security issues, both in developed and developing countries. He has been the editor of several volumes of the *World Labour Report*. His latest publication is an edited volume entitled *Government and its Employees: Case Studies of Developing Countries*.

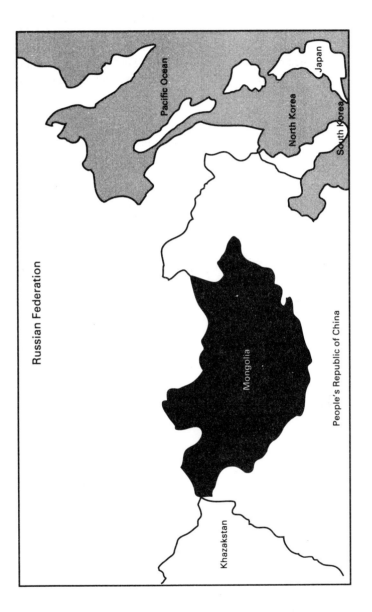

MAP 1   Mongolia's position in Asia

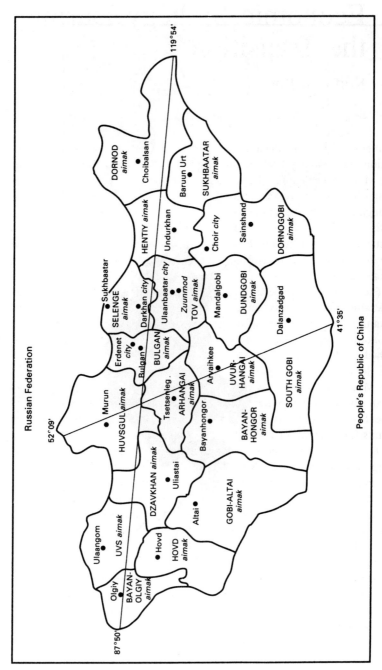

MAP 2   Administrative units of Mongolia

1 Economic Strategy During the Transition

Keith Griffin

Mongolia for many decades was an economic colony of the Soviet Union. The country became independent in 1921 and three years later the Mongolian People's Republic was declared. Mongolia thereby became the first country to follow in the footsteps of the Soviet Union. Mongolia remained a single-party state closely allied to the Soviet Union until early 1990, when demonstrations in March of that year led to the first multi-party elections, the introduction of a new constitution and the beginning of a transition from a centrally-planned to a market-guided economy.

The transition has been difficult, but one should not forget that considerable progress was achieved during the socialist period. Central planning was introduced after the Second World War and a system of economic management closely based on the Soviet model was established. A Friendship and Mutual Assistance Treaty was signed with the Soviet Union in 1946 and in 1962 Mongolia joined the Council for Mutual Economic Assistance (CMEA), the Soviet trade bloc. By 1988 about 93 per cent of the country's trade was with the CMEA. The Soviet Union provided large amounts of foreign aid, either as grants (until 1980) or in the form of concessional loans (from 1981 to 1991). It also integrated the Mongolian economy into the Soviet planning system, providing Mongolia with a large market for her exports, a secure supply of required imports and exceptionally favourable terms of trade. The preferential price for imported oil was especially important and this induced Mongolia to create a structure of production which, for a developing country, is unusually intensive in the use of imported fuel. The Soviet Union also provided a huge amount of technical assistance, including large numbers of senior technical advisers located in all the major ministries.

The development strategy followed by Mongolia during the socialist era was of the classic Soviet type. Priority was given to industry and mining and, within industry, priority was given to intermediate

1

and capital goods industry; consumer goods industries, including agricultural processing, were relatively neglected. The pattern of industrialisation was very capital-intensive and hence relatively little industrial employment was created.[1] Industry was geographically concentrated in Ulaanbaatar and two other cities, and hence few of the benefits of industrialisation reached the countryside. The industrial enterprises were large state monopolies; there were no small enterprises, let alone anything that could be described as a private, informal sector.

Agriculture was starved of investment. A few state farms were created and these were highly mechanised, generating little employment. The internal terms of trade were unfavourable to the rural economy and the large, nomadic livestock sector was largely ignored. Indeed, prices received by rural producers 'remained virtually unchanged for three decades, until 1991'.[2] On the other hand, institutional arrangements were transformed, collectives were created, very good health, education and veterinary services were provided and an excellent safety-net was put in place. The rural sector was physically isolated from the rest of the economy, and remains so to this day. There is only one north–south rail line; there are very few roads and only 3 per cent of the roads (or 1303 km) are paved.[3] The provincial capitals are connected to Ulaanbaatar by fairly frequent (and, until recently, heavily subsidised) air-links, but most overland transport is by horse and camel.

The development strategy seen as a whole was highly inefficient, highly dependent on imports and highly dependent on Soviet aid to finance investment. A substantial part of the industrial sector probably had negative value added when measured at world prices.[4] The economy was very open – imports accounted for 52 per cent of gross domestic product in 1989 – but it was not exposed to world competition because of the very close integration into the Soviet trading bloc. Indeed, over 80 per cent of Mongolia's trade was with the Soviet Union alone. The level of investment was high, but part of the advantage of a high level of investment was offset by a very high capital–output ratio, i.e by a low productivity of investment.

Despite all of this, net material product (NMP) grew 6.4 per cent a year from 1950 to 1985. The share of industry in NMP increased from 7 per cent in 1940 to 35 per cent in 1985. Agriculture, however, grew less rapidly than the population and its share in NMP fell from 77 per cent in 1940 to only 20 per cent in 1985.[5]

The most impressive achievements of the socialist period are the improvements in human development indicators.[6] Life expectancy increased from 46.7 years in 1960 to 62.5 years in 1990. Adult literacy rose to 93 per cent. Virtually the entire population had access to health services; 98 per cent of pregnant women received pre-natal care; 87 per cent of one-year-old children were immunised against disease; malnutrition was rare. On average, Mongolians received seven years of formal education, with girls receiving nearly as much education (6.8 years) as boys (7.2 years). Human capital formation evidently was given a high priority and, as a result, Mongolia's level of human development was noticeably higher than one would expect given her level of material development.

Also impressive were the achievements in the sphere of gender equality. Approximately 98 per cent of women were literate and, until the recent transition period, 86 per cent of women were in the labour force. Women accounted for 43 per cent of the graduates from tertiary education and dominated professions such as medicine and education. This is important both because gender equality is desirable in its own right and because there is strong evidence that virtually all indicators of social well-being are highly and positively correlated with improvements in the economic and social status of women.

THE SEQUENCE OF ECONOMIC REFORMS

Mongolia embarked on a transition to a market-guided economy in July 1990, immediately after the first multi-party elections and the formation of a coalition government. There had been some modest reforms in the period 1986–89,[7] but these occurred within the context of a planned economy. Reforms intended to create a new economic system, namely a market economy, had to wait until the introduction of a new political regime. Within a year of the commencement of the transition, however, Mongolia was subjected to three external shocks: an aid shock, a trade shock and a macroeconomic management shock.

Soviet aid was reduced considerably in 1989 and then, in 1991, terminated. This deprived the economy of external resources in the form of concessionary loans that had been used to finance virtually the entire investment programme. It is estimated that this aid shock was equivalent to perhaps as much as 30 per cent of gross national product. Also in 1991, the Council for Mutual Economic Assistance collapsed, thereby imposing a trade shock on Mongolia. The country suddenly lost its export market and in addition suffered a sharp deterioration in its external terms of trade. In fact it has been claimed that the disintegration of the Soviet trading bloc caused Mongolia to suffer the 'largest decline in terms of trade among the former members of the Council'.[8] This trade shock led to a steep fall in the value of Mongolia's total exports (from US$ 739.1 million in 1988 to US$ 348 million in 1991) and imposed a severe foreign exchange constraint on the economy. Indeed, by 1993 recorded exports still had not recovered their previous peak and were only slightly higher (at US$ 360.9 million) than the 1991 low point. Compounding these difficulties was the third shock, a macroeconomic management shock created by the exodus of senior technical advisers from the Soviet Union. The management of state expenditure on investment and production, whether within a central planning framework or not, suddenly became more difficult as the Mongolians were left without experienced people to help them run the economy. That is, the capacity of the government to manage a development strategy suddenly became weaker just as the transition to a new economic system began.

It is hardly surprising therefore that the transition to a market economy did not proceed smoothly. Inflation soared, average incomes fell sharply and poverty, which had previously been unknown in Mongolia, suddenly became a serious social problem. Table 1.1 contains data on rates of inflation, gross domestic product, GDP per capita and GNP per capita, all expressed as index numbers based on 1989, the last year before the transition began.

As can be seen in the table, inflation, which had been absent in 1989 and 1990, suddenly became very rapid in 1991, the first full year of the transition. The general consumer price index rose 54.3 per cent in 1991, accelerated by 321.1 per cent in 1992 and rose by a further 193 per cent in 1993. These figures, if anything, understate the explosive rise in prices since the consumer price index for 1991 and 1992 included in several cases controlled prices rather than the higher free-market prices. Whatever the 'correct' figures for the rate of inflation might be, there is no doubt that the government lost control of the macroeconomy and created a financial emergency. By the end of the first quarter of 1994, the rate of inflation, although still very high, had been reduced to 80–100 per cent per annum.

The 'real' economy also performed poorly. Gross domestic product per head, based on estimates prepared by the International Monetary Fund, declined in each of the first four years of the transition and at the time of writing in July 1994 it is thought that it possibly will decline again over the whole of 1994. The IMF estimates, moreover, are conservative since they incorporate arbitrary but probably sensible upward adjustments for livestock production and the value of unre-

TABLE 1.1   Inflation and growth, 1989–93

	1989	1990	1991	1992	1993
1. Consumer price index	100	100	154.3	649.8	1838.7
2. Gross domestic product	100	98	90	82	81
3. GDP per capita	100	95	84	77	75
4. GNP per capita	100	95	84	78	70

Notes: The consumer price index in the table is the general CPI.
Rows 2 and 3 are estimates prepared by the IMF.
Row 4 is the official State Statistical Office estimate.

corded trading activities. The truth is that the national accounts of Mongolia are unreliable and there is an urgent need to improve the government's statistical services. Be that as it may, the IMF data suggest that average output and incomes per head declined by five per cent in 1990, by 11.6 per cent in 1991, by 8.3 per cent in 1992 and by a further 2.6 per cent in 1993. The decline in average income over the entire period 1989–93 was about a quarter.[9] Other indicators, as we shall see in other chapters, also point to a dramatic decline in the standard of living of the population.

The financial instability, declining output and deteriorating living conditions caught both the government and the international financial institutions by surprise. Everyone was too optimistic; everyone believed that privatisation of state enterprises combined with the 'magic' of the market would bring rapid, if not instantaneous improvements. In 1991 the government thought output would fall only 5 per cent in 1992; in fact GDP fell 8.9 per cent. It thought the decline in output would cease in 1993; in fact GDP fell 1.2 per cent. In 1991, the government expected growth to be 3 per cent per annum from 1994 onwards whereas growth rates, even if at last they become positive, are unlikely in 1994 to exceed the rate of growth of the population.[10] Assessments have now become more sober and it is 'generally acknowledged that the economic transition was more difficult than had been foreseen'.[11]

A sober assessment of the situation, although welcome, still leaves unanswered a central question: why did incomes fall and poverty increase so dramatically? Three different answers are possible, each with different implications for policy initiatives to alleviate poverty and hardship during the transition.

First, some have argued that Mongolia's difficulties are due to the three external shocks described above. There is no doubt that these shocks – the loss of capital inflows, the decline in the terms of exchange combined with the loss of well-established export markets, and the termination of technical assistance – constituted a severe blow to the economy. Any country subjected to such unfavourable economic developments would have run into serious problems. The question is not whether the external shocks lowered the growth rate and depressed incomes, but whether economic policy and other external events aggravated or diminished the effects of the shocks.

There were, of course, offsetting economic stimuli. These include (i) a large inflow of foreign aid from Western donor countries and international financial institutions, which in terms of commitments were equivalent to about 15 per cent of GDP in 1991 and 1992 or half of the maximum shortfall in Soviet assistance;[12] (ii) the suspension of debt-servicing payments on the large (10.5 billion transferable rubles) Soviet debt; (iii) a large increase in technical assistance financed by multilateral and bilateral aid agencies and international non-governmental organisations; and (iv) an improvement in the quality and diversity of imported goods (particularly imported capital goods) which, after a lag and if effectively exploited, could have raised the productivity of investment.

The increase in Western capital aid and technical assistance was dramatic. In 1990 aid disbursements were $4.7 million. In 1991 they were $80.8 million.[13] They jumped again to $299.2 million in 1992 and then fell to an estimated $104.2 million in 1993. This should have provided a substantial cushion and enabled Mongolia to absorb the external shocks.[14] The improvement in the quality of imports could not compensate for the steep decline in the volume of imports, but had scarce foreign exchange been used to sustain investment rather than consumption, the initial fall in production could have been contained and the rate of growth of output and incomes could have recovered quickly. Had this been done, the rise in poverty would have been smaller in magnitude and shorter in duration.

Perhaps the clinching piece of evidence that external shocks are not entirely to blame for Mongolia's economic difficulties is that output began to decline and poverty began to increase in 1990, a year before the full impact of the external shocks was felt. Net material product declined 4 per cent in 1990; gross domestic product declined 2 per cent; GDP per capita declined 5 per cent. This coincided not with the external shocks but with the beginning of the economic reform process: the liberalisation of intra-public-sector enterprise pricing and the expansion of operating autonomy (1989), the easing of foreign-exchange surrender requirements (1989), the establishment of two commercial banks (1990), the creation of a two-tiered banking system (1990), and the introduction of a foreign-exchange auction system (1990). This coincidence of liberalisation with economic decline suggests there may be a link between the performance of the economy and economic policies adopted to effect the transition from a planned socialist economy to a market-guided economy.[15]

A second hypothesis to explain the dramatic increase in poverty and fall in average incomes is failure of implementation. According to this view, the transition strategy was well designed but policies were often imperfectly implemented. The solution to the problem therefore is to accelerate the reform process and improve the ability of the government to manage the economy.

This is certainly a more plausible view. The combination of external shocks and weaknesses in implementation may suffice to explain what happened. Certainly there were weaknesses in implementation. This is hardly surprising given the speed of change, for the pace of restructuring in Mongolia was 'far quicker than in other economies in transition'.[16] In such circumstances, mistakes were bound to be made.

State enterprises were rapidly privatised, but the management of the newly-privatised enterprises often left much to be desired. Indeed the new units often continued to be run by the old managers. State monopolies were transformed into private monopolies, and government policy failed to create a competitive environment or to prevent monopolistic behaviour by efficient regulation. Private commercial banking was encouraged, but the banks were poorly regulated, lending was often based not on commercial criteria but continued to be directed to favoured enterprises by the political authorities. In some cases state enterprises established banks to provide credit for themselves.[17] In general, 'the weaknesses of the banking sector . . . were . . . underestimated'[18] and both the volume of credit creation and its allocation continue to be major problems.

Prices also were liberalised, but liberalisation was incomplete, subsidies and protection from competition persisted and profitable activities were obstructed by administrative controls. Key food prices, for example, were liberalised only after a substantial lag, thereby creating strong disincentives for rural producers. Both state and privatised industry were shielded from domestic and foreign competition by supplying inputs below cost, allocating foreign exchange at an undervalued rate and, as we have seen, by directing bank credit to them on a preferential basis. Commercial activities and trading were not initially fully privatised; instead the government used its control over marketing and the allocation of credit and fuel to squeeze livestock producers, perhaps in the mistaken belief that the rural sector is less poor than the urban. Power and energy continue to be heavily subsidised both for urban households and industry. Air transport also is heavily subsidised, as are telecommunications. Almost none of these subsidies benefit the poor, none encourage an efficient use of resources and none promote investment and growth. Despite the acute shortage of foreign exchange, export licensing was used to discourage exports of agricultural raw materials and agricultural products and an outright ban was imposed on the export of cashmere. This, too, introduced a bias against the poor. It also encouraged smuggling, for example, of wool. Again, despite the shortage of capital and foreign exchange, many applications from China to invest in trading activities were rejected. It is no wonder that many observers urged the government to intensify price-liberalisation in order to encourage the growth of employment, correct the strong bias against agriculture and alleviate poverty.[19]

In addition to errors in implementing the privatisation and price-liberalisation programmes, there also were serious errors of macroeconomic management. Mongolia increased its foreign indebtedness massively and in a very short time. In 1990 its debt-service ratio was zero, but by 1993 it had risen to 20.1 per cent of export earnings. Mongolia fell into arrears on some of its non-Russian international debt obligations and the country no longer is able to borrow commercially abroad. This might not have mattered if foreign borrowing had been used to finance investment and accelerate growth, but it was used instead to try to sustain an unsustainable level of consumption, as government officials now agree.

To make matters worse, the country's foreign exchange reserves were seriously mismanaged. Either through corruption or incompetence US $17.1 million was squandered on phantom projects and in addition, most of the foreign exchange reserves disappeared.[20] The 'serious deterioration in macroeconomic management'[21] led the Asian Development Bank, the World Bank and the International Monetary Fund temporarily to suspend lending in the third quarter of 1992.

Macroeconomic mismanagement in that period was not confined to failures to husband foreign exchange reserves, to borrow prudently and to maintain the country's international creditworthiness. It also extended to government monetary, expenditure and tax policies. Credit creation in particular got out of control and this led to an explosive rise in prices which threatened to undermine the entire price liberalisation effort and the transition process as a whole. Credit expansion, in turn, had its roots in a collapse of public-sector tax and expenditure policy and a consequent rise in the fiscal deficit. The problem was largely on the expenditure side of the accounts: tax revenues as a percentage of GDP remained fairly stable, but current expenditure soared from 50.2 per cent of GDP in 1989 to 61.5 per cent in 1992.[22] The government deficit was used not to raise investment and growth rates but to prop up failing enterprises in the state sector and to temper for a short period the fall in private consumption. This macroeconomic mismanagement moved the country to the edge of disaster.

There were, thus, numerous failures of implementation, surely enough to account for the trajectory followed by the economy, especially when external shocks also are considered. Yet there is one awkward fact that suggests that the fundamental problem was not imperfect implementation of a well-designed transition strategy but flaws in the design of the strategy itself. This takes us to the third explanation for the sharp fall in average incomes and the equally sharp rise in the incidence of poverty.

The awkward fact is that Mongolia, Russia and the successor states of the Soviet Union, and the eastern and central European countries that belonged to the Council for Mutual Economic Assistance all followed a broadly similar strategy for the transition to a market economy. Some moved more rapidly than others and some had more coherent policies than others, but they all followed broadly the same path. And they all encountered much the same results: rapid inflation, falling output, rising unemployment, increased poverty and a period of negative growth in per capita income. The outcomes were worse in some countries than in others, but in qualitative terms they were broadly the same. Given this striking coincidence of strategies and outcomes, it strains credulity to claim that in each country the strategy was good but the implementation was poor; something deeper evidently was at fault.

Mongolia, in fact, compares favourably with most of the members of the Commonwealth of Independent States and with the other countries that once were part of the Soviet bloc. Despite external shocks and faulty policy implementation, inflation rose less rapidly and output declined less sharply than in most other countries going through a transition from one economic system to another. The difference in performance is probably due to the exceptionally large amount of foreign assistance received by Mongolia (in comparison to the other Soviet-bloc countries) and the resilience of the largely self-provisioning livestock sector. Even so, economic performance left much to be desired and the reason, we believe, has to do with the general strategy followed.

The strategy is revealed by the sequence of reforms and by the emphasis given to implementing the various reforms. The strategy followed in Mongolia, and in many other former Soviet-bloc countries, is popularly known as the 'big bang' or as 'shock therapy'. The essence of the big bang is a rapid transformation of property relations, i.e. privatisation of state enterprises, accompanied by an equally rapid dismantling of administrative controls, i.e. price-liberalisation. This is the strategy that was adopted in Mongolia.

It is widely recognised that privatisation of the state-owned enterprises was 'at the center of the reform program',[23] and many senior government officials regard the most important achievement of the reform process as finding a solution to the 'property issue'. Equally, price-liberalisation was given very high priority. Consider the timing of the reforms. Privatisation began in October 1991, just three months after the formation of a coalition government. A stock exchange was created a few months later, in 1992, although a secondary market in equities has not yet emerged. By the end of 1993, some 2440 small enterprises had been privatised and 797 large ones, for a total of 3237 enterprises transformed in whole or in part to private ownership.[24] Supporters of the programme claim the results have been 'impressive' and that Mongolia has had 'the most successful privatization program as compared to other programs in effect in Republics of the former Soviet Union'.[25] We shall examine the privatisation programme in greater detail below, but the statement that privatisation was 'at the center' of the reform process is undoubtedly true.

Price-liberalisation was the second leg of the transition strategy. Selected retail prices were freed, i.e. raised, in 1990. Retail prices were raised again in 1991. The great majority of prices were deregulated in 1992. A private banking system was created in embryo in 1990 and commercial banking reforms were accelerated in 1991. The tugrik was devalued in 1991. The result was rapid inflation and the government was forced to raise wages and pensions in partial compensation. The latter added to inflation. Although nominal interest rates were raised in 1991 and again in 1992, they remained highly negative in both years in real terms, further contributing to the monetary disarray. In an attempt to reduce the macroeconomic disequilibrium, the government in 1992 reduced budget transfers to its wholly- and partially-owned enterprises, but the state enterprises responded by seeking and obtaining huge injections of credit from the commercial banking system, thereby defeating the purpose of government policy.

By then macroeconomic policy was in a complete mess. The government had lost control of monetary policy. The commercial banking system was unregulated but subject to arbitrary interference. Credit-creation was rampant. Negative real interest rates discouraged saving and encouraged capital-intensive methods of production, and hence discouraged employment creation. The average price level was rising rapidly and changes in relative prices were arbitrary, depending on the timing of individual price changes. The price mechanism thus was unable to perform its allocative function effectively and hence potential efficiency gains were lost. Production and average incomes declined. Unemployment rose. Poverty increased. Savings fell sharply and became negligible. The capacity of the country to finance investment and growth virtually disappeared and the rate of growth of per capita income became negative. The country was kept afloat by foreign aid.

This reading of the evidence thus traces Mongolia's difficulties not to failures of implementation but to a poorly-designed strategy, and specifically to an incorrect sequence of reforms. Poverty arose because of strategic errors, i.e. because of wrong priorities. The key mistake, the fatal flaw, was to make privatisation the top priority.

PRIVATISATION: A CRITIQUE

The role of privatisation in the transition to a market economy has been greatly exaggerated, to the detriment of the people whose livelihoods are at stake. Privatisation is essentially an ideological issue and is not necessary for the creation of a well-functioning market-guided economy. Depending on one's political preferences, one can envisage a socialist market economy (as is being created in China), a mixed economy with a substantial public sector (as exists in much of Western Europe) or an economy dominated by private enterprise (as exists in the United States). A market economy is compatible with many different distributions of property rights between the public and private sectors.

That being so, there is no economic reason to put privatisation 'at the center of the reform program', as was done in Mongolia. Indeed, privatisation should be given a low priority during the transition process and government effort should be directed to those issues on which the success of the transition ultimately depends. Even if government intends to dispose of most public-sector enterprises, the timing of the transfer of ownership should be treated pragmatically so that policymakers can concentrate on doing first things first. Privatisation is largely an irrelevance when designing a transition strategy.

The success of the transition depends on three things: (i) creating an environment in which the market mechanism can operate efficiently, (ii) maintaining and preferably accelerating the rate of growth so that reform is accompanied by a rise in the average standard of living and (iii) constructing an effective social safety-net or welfare system so that those who are harmed by restructuring the economy are not thrown into poverty. A privatisation programme should be judged by whether it contributes to these three objectives. In the case of Mongolia, privatisation has failed on every count. Why is this so?

Privatisation is concerned with the transfer of property rights. Such a transfer in itself implies neither an increase in efficiency nor an acceleration of growth nor the protection of those threatened by poverty. It all depends on the circumstances. Let us examine the circumstances in Mongolia.

Privatisation in Mongolia was implemented by distributing vouchers to the entire population, red ones for small state enterprises and blue ones for large. The red vouchers were used in bidding for small firms at auction while the blue vouchers were used to acquire shares in large joint-stock companies through batch sales on the stock exchange. Privatisation in Mongolia was a pure transfer scheme: the government distributed state assets to private citizens. This transfer scheme presumably resulted initially in a highly equitable distribution of wealth, but it did little to increase economic efficiency or improve the allocative function of the markets for goods and services. Ownership is diffuse, shareholders exercise little control over management (who usually are the same persons who managed the state enterprise before privatisation), financial accountability is poor, and many of the large 'privatised' enterprises continue to have majority (15.8 per cent) or minority (8.4 per cent) state ownership. In practice, 'shareholders have control only in theory but against a background of zero real ownership'.[26] Equally important, privatisation has not led to greater competition, lower costs and allocative efficiency. Because of the very small domestic market in Mongolia, privatised enterprises are able to exercise monopoly power as sellers and for companies purchasing products from the rural areas, 'there is almost a monopsonistic buying arrangement'.[27]

Privatisation has so far been equally irrelevant in terms of stimulating faster growth. Because state enterprise and collective assets were given away rather than sold, there was no incentive for would-be owners to save in order to accumulate assets. Private wealth increased without the necessity of private effort and, if anything, the windfall gain in wealth probably depressed private savings behaviour. Those who sold their red vouchers on the secondary market (at a 70 per cent discount, on average) used the proceeds to sustain consumption; those who retained their vouchers acquired assets at zero cost. Privatisation thus had a zero or negative effect on the aggregate rate of savings and hence did nothing to increase the rate of growth during the delicate period of the transition from one economic regime to another. Moreover, the new owners of the privatised enterprises have so far failed to invest in their own companies and hence there have been few microeconomic efficiency gains at the level of the firm and no expansion of output after the transfer of property rights. Private entrepreneurship in Mongolia has focused on trading activities rather than production.

Lastly, and unsurprisingly, privatisation has had no role to play in constructing a social safety-net or in preventing the emergence of serious poverty. If it has had any effect, it must have been negative since the state enterprises and rural collectives provided secure employment to their workers and a range of social benefits. Employment in the newly-privatised enterprises is much less secure, redundant labour has been dismissed and unemployment has risen. Unit costs have in some cases been cut, and losses diminished or profits increased, but this has been achieved by transferring the costs of higher unemployment on to society at large. Microeconomic efficiency may have increased in some cases, but this occurred at the expense of macroeconomic efficiency.

Privatisation thus was a partial administrative success, in the sense that a formal transfer of ownership did indeed occur, but it appears to have been an economic failure. It did nothing positive to assist Mongolia through the transition difficulties and, by creating private monopolies, undermining savings and accentuating unemployment, it had several negative effects. Instead of privatising existing assets, the government would have been well-advised to concentrate on creating conditions for new enterprises to emerge in the private sector. What is desperately needed is not a redistribution of wealth from the public to the private sector but the creation of new wealth by creating space in which a dynamic private sector can accumulate, innovate and grow. The emphasis given to privatisation was and continues to be a tragic waste of time. Even the World Bank, an outspoken champion of the private sector, has begun to have doubts. As it says, 'Experience . . . suggests that perhaps excessive reliance is being placed on the role of privatization relative to other reforms.'[28]

AN ALTERNATIVE STRATEGY

What are these 'other reforms' that experience suggests merit higher priority for government policy? Is there an alternative sequence of reforms that could yield better results? We believe there is.

The point of departure for a successful transition to a market economy is recognition that price stabilisation is a *sine qua non*. Market economies work well only if market signals are accurate indicators of costs and benefits. If prices fail to reflect social costs and benefits, the market mechanism will not lead to an efficient allocation of resources and it will not allocate investment expenditure to the socially most profitable economic activities. The level of output and incomes consequently will be lower than they might have been and the rate of growth will be slower. The incidence of poverty will be higher than would otherwise be necessary and the time required to eradicate poverty will be longer.

Success in a market economy depends on the ability of enterprises and households to respond quickly to changes in relative prices. If inflation is rapid, however, changes in relative prices become blurred, masked by the change in the average level of prices. Moreover, changes in relative prices become arbitrary and temporary, affected by the vagaries in timing of price-changes in specific markets, and this makes it difficult for enterprises and households to interpret market-signals correctly. The result is greater risk for investors, generalised uncertainty for everyone and a slowing down in the pace of economic activity. It is for these reasons that uncontrolled inflation poses the greatest threat to a successful transition to a market economy.

Macroeconomic stabilisation should therefore be the top priority.[29] In practice this implies that the government should take whatever steps are necessary to balance the public accounts (including imposing financial constraints on state enterprises) combined with a firm monetary policy that ensures that both borrowers and depositors face significantly positive real rates of interest. During this stabilisation period the banking system should not be privatised since excessive credit creation during the transition to a market economy would likely result in either open or suppressed inflation depending on the extent of price-liberalisation. Thus tax reform, expenditure reform and interest-rate reform should take the lead, complemented by the creation of effective market institutions.

Unfortunately, this did not occur in Mongolia. Tax reform (the introduction of a sales tax) came too late to prevent the emergence of huge fiscal deficits. The state enterprises were not confronted by a hard budget constraint but first were subsidised directly by the central government and later by state-directed credit allocations from the banking system. Hence even when the government's accounts moved into surplus (in early 1994), the money supply continued to increase rapidly because credit continued to be directed to both the privatised and remaining state enterprises. Nominal interest rates on loans and deposits were well below the rate of inflation from 1991 to 1993, although in 1994 the real loan-rate of interest swung to the opposite extreme and became absurdly high while the real deposit-rate of interest has become moderately positive. It was a serious error to create a private commercial banking system before the economy was stabilised. The authorities lost control of credit creation and an explosion in prices was the result. A top priority now should be to impose control over the commercial banking system (if necessary by taking some banks into public ownership) and to complete the interest rate reforms.

There are frequent complaints in Mongolia that credit is scarce, that tight monetary policy is preventing the expansion of the private sector and that special credit programmes should be established for small businesses as a way to alleviate poverty. These arguments are almost entirely fallacious. Credit is abundant and monetary policy is still loose; the problem is not a low volume of credit but an allocation of credit that responds to arbitrary political interference and personal private connections rather than to commercial criteria. New (and potentially efficient) firms cannot obtain credit because the old (and largely inefficient) firms have managed to secure control (directly and indirectly) over the credit-creating institutions. The solution is not to create special credit schemes for seemingly deserving groups of borrowers, but to move ahead quickly with bank regulation, the creation of a system of commercial law and the development of institutional mechanisms for the enforcement of contracts.

Meanwhile, much of the private sector – agriculture, small-scale industry, trading and the informal sector – should be encouraged to self-finance their current activities and their expansion plans. This, after all, is the way the private sector has developed in most countries. This implies that informal financial institutions (money-lenders, the 'curb' market, trade credit) should be openly tolerated and that formal sector non-bank private financial institutions should be allowed to emerge. This is far more important than creating a deposit-taking private commercial banking system. A policy of self-finance for most of the private sector, however, requires a set of incentives, including positive real rates of interest, which encourage savings while simultaneously reflecting the true scarcity of capital.

The problem is that real incomes are still falling and hence the ability of the population to save and self-finance small and informal sector enterprises is severely limited. Until growth rates become positive and average incomes start to rise, private sector savings are likely to remain low. Reform of the banking system and a reallocation of credit to sectors where finance capital can most profitably be used will probably take some time. Poverty, also, is rising rapidly and something must be done quickly. We are therefore left with little alternative but to create special *ad hoc* funds to address urgent poverty issues. (See Chapters 2 and 6.) But the creation of special credit programmes should be regarded as very definitely second-best policies. The first-best policy is to stabilise prices, improve the allocation of credit through the financial system and ensure that interest rates are moderately positive in real terms.

Next in order of priority are measures intended to stimulate growth. Macroeconomic stabilisation is not an end in itself: the purpose of stability is to create an environment favourable to the expansion of output and incomes and to the efficient operation of the price mechanism. Mongolia so far has failed to achieve either stabilisation or growth of its economy. The crucial mistake was to respond to the external shocks by attempting to maintain consumption standards rather than to restructure the economy by using a high rate of investment to grow out of inefficiency. The reluctance or inability to increase taxation, the use of the fiscal deficit to sustain high levels of current government expenditure, and the negative real rates of interest in the early years of the transition conspired to raise consumption at the expense of savings and investment. Gross domestic savings in 1989 are estimated to have been 13 per cent of GDP. A year later they had collapsed to 3.1 per cent.[30] Today, in 1994, net savings may well still be negative, the low rate of positive net private sector savings offset by dis-saving in the public and quasi-public sectors. Thus the macroeconomic balance between consumption and investment is strongly biased against growth. As a result, the population has grown faster than output and poverty has increased.

A further mistake as regards growth was to pursue rapid price-liberalisation across the board. It would have been more sensible to liberalise more selectively and more gradually, beginning in those sectors where the prospects for fast growth were most promising and with those prices which are of strategic importance. In Mongolia this implies liberalising agriculture and trade (domestic and foreign) first and then using the growth momentum generated in those two sectors to extend the reforms to industry and the rest of the economy. Instead price-liberalisation in agriculture lagged behind the rest of the economy and controls over exports remained in place – particularly controls over agricultural exports – long after other controls were removed. The strategic prices in an agriculture-led growth strategy were (i) livestock and livestock product prices, (ii) the real exchange rate and (iii) the real rate of interest.

In each case relative prices moved in the opposite direction from that required by an efficient growth strategy. The internal terms of trade were turned against agriculture and in favour of industry. Yet the short-term prospects for industrial growth were poor, partly because of the large capital requirements for industrial expansion and partly because of the structural inefficiency of the industrial sector and the existence of many enterprises with negative value added. Large parts of agriculture, e.g. cashmere and wool, could have been competitive in world markets; most of industry could not. A competitive livestock sector, however, required a favourable real exchange rate.

Unfortunately, the nominal exchange rate (tugriks per US dollar) did not keep up with inflation and as a result the tugrik became severely overvalued. The real exchange rate (i.e. the nominal rate adjusted for inflation) moved erratically but fairly systematically against exporters. (See Table 1.2.) It was not until May 1993, when a unified and floating rate of exchange was introduced, that the real rate stabilised and even began to provide a positive incentive to export.

TABLE 1.2   Nominal and real exchange rate, 1985–94

	Nominal rate	Real rate (index: 1985 = 100)
1985	3.7	100
1989	3.0	80.4
1990	4.3	112.6
1991	8.0	171.9
1992	35.8	273.1
1993	294.4	549.9
1994	401.3	488.8

Source: International Monetary Fund.

The interest rate, as we have seen, discouraged savings by depositors and encouraged those who obtained credit to use capital wastefully. The real deposit rate of interest was slightly positive in 1989 and 1990 but then became negative in 1991, falling to a horrific minus 224.3 per cent per annum in 1993. In 1994 the rate of inflation began to fall while nominal deposit rates continued to rise and as a result in January the real rate of interest on deposits became positive again, at a moderate 11 per cent per annum. Real lending rates were negative from 1991 to 1993, thereby providing a massive subsidy to borrowers. In January 1994 they rose dramatically to +161 per cent a year, a level which clearly exceeds the normal return on investment and which therefore cannot be sustained. (See Table 1.3.) Extremely high real rates of interest are as damaging to growth as extremely low real rates of interest.

The inescapable conclusion is that the liberalisation process damaged growth prospects and helped to accentuate poverty. The wrong sectors were given favourable treatment and the key prices for growth were allowed to lag behind the rate of inflation and thus to give the wrong signals to an economy urgently in need of expansion. The 'big bang' caused the economy to implode rather than to explode in dynamism and growth. Indeed the attempt to liberalise (almost) all prices at once paradoxically led many economic agents to retreat from the market economy. In the rural areas many households reduced their market orientation and relied on self-provisioning; the result in the cities was a scarcity of supplies. The unfavourable terms of trade confronting the livestock sector and the instability and unpredictability of relative prices led many to abandon market exchange and retreat into barter exchange, with resulting inefficiencies arising from diminished specialisation and division of labour. Still others circumvented controls over exports by taking to smuggling, which inevitably raised the costs of engaging in international trade and reduced the volume of exports below what they could have been. An economy starved of foreign exchange after the collapse of the Council for Mutual Economic Assistance adopted trade, foreign-investment and exchange-rate policies which accentuated the hardships of ordinary people. Still others, responding to rampant inflation and negative real rates of interest, retreated from the national currency and increasingly used US dollars as a unit of account, a store of value and a medium of exchange. It became possible to live in Mongolia without ever using and hardly even seeing Mongolian currency. The transition strategy adopted by the government impeded rather than encouraged movement to an efficient market economy.

TABLE 1.3   Nominal and real commercial bank interest rates,
1989–94, in per cent per annum

| | Average lending rate | | Average deposit rate | |
	Nominal	Real	Nominal	Real
1989	5–10	3.8 to 8.8	3–4	1.8 to 2.8
1990	5–10	3.1 to 8.1	3–4	1.1 to 2.1
1991	4–26	−18.7 to +3.3	3–4	−19.7 to −18.7
1992	57.0	−124.1	18.6	−162.5
1993	188.2	−119.0	83.9	−224.3
1994 (Jan.)	245.0	+161	95.0	11.0

Note: The real rate of interest is calculated as the nominal rate of interest minus the annual rate of increase in the general consumer price index.

Source: International Monetary Fund.

Given the faulty strategy, there was little choice but to rely on foreign aid and fortunately aid proved to be forthcoming in substantial volume. It must be recognised, however, that large inflows of foreign aid during a transition process can be a double-edged sword. On the one hand, aid can help maintain the standard of living during a period of stress and help to contain the rise in poverty. On the other hand, if aid inflows increase substantially at the same time that foreign trade is being liberalised, they will tilt the exchange rate in the wrong direction and provide incorrect long-term price signals. This will occur by turning relative prices against exports and import-competing products, depressing the relative price of internationally-traded goods and diverting investment into non-tradeables such as housing and restaurants. Worse, if aid inflows are used to sustain consumption rather than investment, debt-servicing problems will be created for the future – unless, of course, all of the aid is in the form of grants. In general, heavy reliance on foreign aid is likely to make the transition to a market economy more difficult rather than less. It is much better to encourage domestic savings and the emergence of a self-financed private sector.

It is here, as we have stressed, that the emphasis on privatisation was misplaced. The pressing need during the transition is to create opportunities for new firms to be created by private entrepreneurial initiative. Ideally these firms should be small, highly competitive and employment-intensive. If small-scale private enterprise takes off and grows rapidly, the share of state enterprises in total production will decline automatically without the necessity to alter property rights. Privatisation should be postponed until the economy has achieved stability, growth has resumed and space has been created for a dynamic private sector to emerge spontaneously.

Lastly, a welfare system or social safety-net should be constructed to assist those who are harmed in the process of restructuring the economy. The number of people falling into poverty and hence who need to be caught in the net should be relatively small if the transition strategy is properly designed. Stabilisation of the macroeconomy should prevent the massive disruption caused by uncontrolled inflation. An emphasis on investment and growth should ensure that average incomes rise. And the creation of space for the emergence of small-scale, labour-intensive private sector activities should ensure that growth is accompanied by a rapid increase in employment and a rise in the real incomes of workers. The social safety-net should therefore have to deal only with the residual, i.e. those who are poor because of special circumstances: the ill, the elderly and the infirm; orphaned children and female-headed households with many dependants; those who are unemployable because of physical or mental handicaps; those who are temporarily unemployed because they lack the skills needed to prosper in the labour market or because of frictions, rigidities or other malfunctionings in the economy; and those who are seasonally unemployed because of the climate-determined nature of much rural activity.

If the transition strategy is flawed and, say, one person in four falls into poverty, it will be difficult for the safety-net to cope. If there are only three persons out of poverty for every one person in poverty, it is unlikely that solidarity within the community will be strong enough to sustain the sacrifices of the non-poor that will be necessary to lift the poor over the poverty threshold. But if the transition strategy can reduce the number in poverty to, say, 10 per cent, there will then be nine persons out of poverty for every person in poverty. A carefully constructed social safety-net should be able to deal with poverty of this order of magnitude, even in a country such as Mongolia, where the average level of income is low and the distribution of income is relatively equal. It is for this reason that the foundation of a poverty-alleviation programme in Mongolia should be sustained growth that is evenly distributed among the entire population.

SUMMARY AND CONCLUSIONS

The transition to a market economy in Mongolia has proved to be more difficult than was originally anticipated. Inflation has been very rapid, per capita income has declined by about 25 per cent and poverty has risen dramatically. The government, evidently, lost control of the macroeconomy.

One explanation for the poor economic performance is the series of external shocks suffered by the economy: the termination of Soviet aid, the withdrawal of Soviet advisers and the collapse of the Soviet trading bloc, CMEA. While these undoubtedly were serious blows, there were a number of offsetting external stimuli which cushioned the blows: a large inflow of financial aid from other sources, suspension of debt-servicing on Soviet loans, provision of technical assistance by a number of donors, and greater diversity in trading partners and hence an improvement in the quality of imports.

Mongolia is strategically well-placed to benefit from the rapidly expanding markets in China, Japan and the rest of east Asia; and when the Russian economy revives, Mongolia is well-placed to export to that market too. The collapse of the CMEA – which accounted for over 90 per cent of Mongolia's trade prior to the transition and little more than half in 1993 – is really a blessing in disguise.

A second explanation for the difficulties encountered during the transition places emphasis on failures of implementation of economic policy. Here again, there is some merit for this view. There were errors in implementing the privatisation programme. There were serious mistakes in monetary policy: an excessive volume of credit was created and the allocation of credit among enterprises was poor. Fiscal policy, too, ran into problems: government current expenditure rose sharply in the early years in order to support loss-making enterprises and this resulted in extraordinarily large public-sector deficits The price-liberalisation programme was only partially complete and heavy subsidies to some activities remained. There was excessive foreign commercial borrowing and the country's foreign exchange reserves were mismanaged.

The fundamental problem, however, was not implementation but major flaws in the design of the transition strategy. The sequence of reforms was incorrect; the government chose the wrong priorities.

The key error was to give first priority to the rapid transformation of property relations. Privatisation of state enterprises should not have been placed at the centre of the reform effort because whether or not privatisation is successful, it has relatively little to do with the creation of an efficient market-guided economy. Further privatisation of state enterprises and of the stock of state-owned urban housing should be postponed until the transition is complete and policy-makers should turn their attention to more pressing issues.[31]

A second flaw in the design of the transition strategy was to dismantle controls and push ahead with rapid price-liberalisation before macroeconomic stability had been achieved. The results were very rapid inflation (which severely weakened the ability of the market mechanism to allocate resources efficiently) and negative real rates of interest (which damaged incentives to save and distorted the allocation of capital).

A related flaw was the premature creation of a private commercial banking system. This helped to fuel inflation and increase instability, and it made it harder for the government to organise an orderly transition to a market economy. The priorities now should be to regain control of the banking system by introducing legislation for bank regulation, developing a system of commercial law and establishing a mechanism for the enforcement of contracts.

There are three essential elements in a successful transition strategy: (i) macroeconomic stabilisation to create an environment in which the market mechanism can operate effectively, (ii) sustained growth based on high savings rates and investment in physical and human capital and (iii) a social safety-net to assist those who would otherwise fall into poverty.

Top priority in Mongolia today should be to complete the stabilisation programme. This implies, first, institutionalising moderate but positive real rates of interest for loans and deposits, establishing control over the banking system and substituting commercial criteria for government interventions when allocating credit.

It also implies, second, further reform of public sector expenditure policies. There is a need to impose a hard budget constraint on public-sector enterprises, as the government intends. There is a need to adopt benefit–cost analysis when evaluating public-sector investment projects, so that projects with negative value-added (such as the new steel-mill) do not absorb very scarce capital resources. And there is a need to reallocate public spending in favour of human capital formation and a social safety-net. It is striking, for example, that in 1993 military spending accounted for 12.6 per cent of government current expenditure whereas the social safety-net was allocated only 0.4 per cent.[32] The situation is less bad in the draft budget for 1994, but even so, military spending is planned to be more than twice as large as spending on all social services combined. Might not Mongolia take advantage of its strategic location as a buffer state and follow Costa Rica's example by eliminating its armed forces? The point is that if the reduction of poverty, and preferably its elimination, is to receive the highest priority, as we believe it should, all items of public expenditure, without exception, will have to be reconsidered from the point of view of its impact on the level of poverty. (An institutional mechanism for doing this is discussed in Chapter 10.)

Third, stabilisation implies further tax reforms. The government needs additional revenue to finance essential investments in infrastructure (power and communications) and human capital, and it will have to spend more on a social safety-net. Given the need to encourage savings, the tax system should be designed whenever possible to discourage consumption and to promote investment, savings and growth. Obvious candidates for a heavier tax burden are an extension of the sales tax, an eventual introduction of a value-added tax, high excise taxes on alcohol and other luxuries, introduction of grazing fees on public land and a slightly higher revenue tariff on imports.

Let us turn next to the second essential element in a successful transition strategy, namely accelerated growth. The crucial error of the government's strategy was to try to maintain the level of current consumption rather than to sustain investment and growth, and hence increase future consumption. Domestic savings fell from a peak of just over 30 per cent of total income in 1986 to possibly negative values today. This collapse now has to be reversed. Moderately high real rates of interest, as already discussed, have a part to play. So, too, does government tax and expenditure policy, as just mentioned. Unfortunately, the privatisation programme was implemented in such a way that savings were discouraged, but if the suggestion is accepted that privatisation of public housing and further privatisation of state enterprises be postponed until after the transition, this negative effect on savings will diminish.

Rather than continue with privatisation, priority should be given to creating conditions for new enterprises to emerge in the private sector. There are numerous administrative obstacles to establishing small, labour-intensive private enterprises and these should be removed as quickly as possible. Specific policy suggestions are discussed in Chapters 3, 6, 7 and 8 below.

Once a favourable environment is created for private entrepreneurial initiative, self-financing of small enterprises becomes a realistic possibility. The government should allow informal financial institutions to emerge and should not erect obstacles to the activities of money lenders, the curb market for credit and the like. Small-scale informal sector lending can play an important part in revitalising the economy. The fact is that the government's 'big bang' strategy backfired; it led to an implosion of the economy rather than to an explosion of growth. One of the consequences was that movement toward a market economy actually was impeded.

Finally, there is the question of foreign aid. There is a danger that must be guarded against that large inflows of external capital will lead to an appreciation of the real rate of exchange. This will turn relative prices against export activities and import-competing products and retard the necessary restructuring of the economy. There is also a danger that large inflows of foreign capital will lower the real rate of interest and in other ways encourage consumption at the expense of savings. A dependence on foreign aid should be avoided, especially since there is no guarantee that high levels of foreign assistance will continue indefinitely. Mongolia should aim for self-reliance and regard foreign aid as a necessary but strictly temporary expedient.

NOTES

1. In 1992 industry accounted for 38.5 per cent of all fixed assets; agriculture for 8.6 per cent. Fixed assets per worker were 151 900 tugriks in industry as compared to 15 700 tugriks in agriculture. (State Statistical Office, *Statistical Yearbook 1993*, Ulaanbaatar, 31 March 1994.) The exchange rate used in this volume is 400 tugriks = US$1.
2. World Bank, *Mongolia: Toward a Market Economy*, Washington, DC, 1992, p. 18.
3. Government of Mongolia, World Bank and the International Monetary Fund, *Mongolia Policy Framework Paper*, 28 May 1993, p. 17.
4. International Labour Office, *Mongolia: Policies for Equitable Transition*, Geneva, November 1992, p. 1.
5. Asian Development Bank, *Mongolia: Economic Reforms and Development Issues*, Manila, 30 April 1992, p. 2.
6. United Nations Development Programme, *Human Development Report 1993* (New York: Oxford University Press, 1993).
7. The dates of the key reforms are listed in World Bank, op. cit., Box 3.1, p. 27.
8. United Nations Development Programme, *Mongolia Poverty Alleviation Strategy, Background Paper*, draft, Ulaanbaatar, December 1993, p. 2.
9. A UNDP estimate, in contrast, suggests that GNP per capita declined by 34 per cent between 1989 and 1992. (See United Nations Development Programme, *Mongolia Background Paper Examining Possible LDC Characteristics*, Ulaanbaatar, June 1993, Table 1, p. 3.) The Asian Development Bank reached a similar conclusion. (See Asian Development Bank, *Mongolia Country Operational Program Paper 1993–1996*, Manila, April 1993, Appendix 1, p. 15.)

10. Even if there is zero growth of GDP in 1994, in conformity with the central forecast, this implies a further fall in per capita income five years after the transition began.
11. Asian Development Bank, ibid., p. ii. Forecasts of the rate of growth of GDP and of exports were persistently overestimated, as were forecasts of the level of foreign aid, both by government and the international agencies. That is, there was excessive optimism, bordering on wishful thinking, all round.
12. United Nations Development Programme, *Mongolia: Aide Memoire on Aid Coordination and Management*, Ulaanbaatar, September 1993.
13. United Nations Development Programme, *Development Co-operation, Mongolia*, 1992 Report, October 1993.
14. Some observers have discounted the significance of Western aid. They argue, first, that a significant portion of the disbursed aid was used to provide spare parts and keep an obsolete infrastructure in working order, notably the power plants, railways and mines. Second, a major part of technical assistance disbursements went toward studies, consultancy reports and the like that were regarded by donors as necessary prerequisites for possible future loans. The short-run benefits of this technical assistance accrued more to the donors than to the economy of Mongolia, although it is conceivable that in the longer term Mongolia will receive more benefit. The question of the possible contributions of foreign aid to poverty alleviation in Mongolia is discussed in Chapter 11.
15. Some have argued, perhaps a bit disingenuously, that the policy failures should themselves be attributed to an external shock, namely, the macroeconomic management shock. Moreover, it is claimed, the Western advisers were as ignorant as their Mongolian colleagues and had to rely on 'guesswork'. This argument ignores the fact that China is on Mongolia's southern border and began the transition from a planned to a market-guided economy in late 1978, or a decade before Mongolia. Guesswork should not have been necessary if for no other reason than there was by 1989 a huge literature on the Chinese experience. The excuse that there was no 'road map' cannot be taken seriously.
16. United Nations Development Programme, *Mongolia: Poverty Alleviation Strategy, Background Paper*, op. cit. p. 2.
17. Asian Development Bank, *Mongolia: Economic Reforms and Development Issues*, op. cit., p. 4.
18. Asian Development Bank, *Mongolia Country Operational Program Paper 1993–1996*, op. cit., p. 9.
19. See, for instance, International Labour Office, op. cit., p. 57. Also see Asian Development Bank, *Mongolia: Economic Reforms and Development Issues*, op. cit., pp. 16–37.
20. Asian Development Bank, ibid., p. 13. The three 1992 phantom projects listed by the Asian Development Bank are a joint venture for camel wool processing with a US firm, a down-payment on a bogus loan of $50 million offered by a German and down-payment for a Boeing 757 airliner.
21. Asian Development Bank, *Mongolia Country Operational Program Paper 1993–1996*, op. cit., p. ii.
22. World Bank, *Mongolia: Toward a Market Economy*, op. cit., Table 2.6, p. 12.

23. Ibid., p. xi.
24. See the World Bank study prepared by Hongjoo Hahm, 'The Status of Privatization', processed, 10 December 1993, Table 4, p. 4. Also see Cevdet Denizer and Alan Gelb, *Mongolia: Privatization and System Transformation in an Isolated Economy*, World Bank, Policy Research Working Papers 1063, December 1992 and Georges Korsun and Peter Murrell, *Ownership and Governance on the Morning After: The Initial Results of Privatization in Mongolia*, Center for Institutional Reform and the Informal Sector (IRIS), Working Paper No. 95, January 1994.
25. Hongjoo Hahm, op cit., p. 5.
26. Ibid., p. 8.
27. Ibid., p. 9.
28. World Bank, *Mongolia: Toward a Market Economy*, op. cit., p. 33.
29. See Ronald I. McKinnon, *The Order of Economic Liberalization* (Baltimore: Johns Hopkins University Press, 2nd edition, 1993) and Keith Griffin and Azizur Rahman Khan, 'The Chinese Transition to a Market-Guided Economy: The Contrast with Russia and Eastern Europe', *Contention*, Vol. 3, no. 2, Winter 1994.
30. World Bank, *Mongolia: Toward a Market Economy*, op. cit., Table 2.4, p. 9.
31. This possibility also is raised by the Asian Development Bank, *Mongolia: Economic Reforms and Development Issues*, op. cit., pp. 28–9, 51.
32. Ibid., p. 15.

2 Poverty: Concepts and Measurement

Keith Griffin

Widespread poverty is a new phenomenon in Mongolia. It did not exist before the country embarked on the transition to a market economy. Indeed poverty is a product partly of external shocks but largely of the transition strategy, a consequence of the policies adopted to convert Mongolia from a centrally planned to a market-guided economy. And judging by the absence of measures to prevent or to contain poverty in the design of the transition strategy, the emergence of poverty as a major issue must have been unanticipated. Poverty caught the policy makers off their guard.

But what exactly is poverty? What do we mean when we say there are so many poor people or that x per cent of the population is living in poverty? Can poverty be measured precisely or quantified in a way that leaves no ambiguities or room for disagreement? Unfortunately, poverty is a social illness; it is not a yes-or-no situation like a medical condition; it is unlike a broken arm or a ruptured appendix which either one does or does not have. Poverty necessarily is a relative concept not an absolute one, but one must still ask, relative to what?

There are three different ways to define poverty. One way – which we shall call income poverty – conceives of poverty as a relationship of a person to a bundle of commodities. In one variant the bundle is disaggregated and specified as a list of 'basic needs' with a threshold or norm established for each basic need, such as a minimum consumption of food, fuel and clothing, a minimum standard for shelter, and so on. 'If for any one of these . . . indicators a household does not meet the selected norm, it is scored as being poor. Poverty is thus a state in which any one of the several basic needs is unsatisfied.'[1] More commonly, the bundle of commodities is aggregated and specified as a minimum living standard or a minimum level of income. Often the minimum level of income – the so-called poverty-line – is based on nutritional standards, e.g. that level of income which is sufficient to prevent malnutrition. In effect, then, the minimum income standard is

27

anchored to one basic need, namely food, which implicitly is regarded as more fundamental or more important than other basic needs.

A second way to view poverty is as a relationship of a person to a set of 'functionings' or 'capabilities'. This approach regards commodities or income not as ends in themselves but as means which enable people to function or to exercise their capabilities. The ultimate objective is capabilities, not income, e.g. the ability to lead a long life, to function without chronic morbidity, to be capable of reading, writing and performing numerical tasks, to be able to move about from place to place, and so on. Some people will require more resources, commodities or income than others to achieve the same capability. For example, a lame person will require more resources (a walking stick, crutches, a wheelchair) than those who are sound of limb to be equally capable of mobility. The resources needed to achieve comparable capabilities may vary across groups as well as between individuals. Women, for example, may have special disadvantages in converting income into capabilities. For instance, because of the demands of pregnancy or nursing an infant, they may encounter nutritional disadvantages; because of job discrimination, they may be less capable of finding satisfying work; because of abandonment by their husbands, they may have special difficulties achieving security. The poor, according to this view, are those whose capabilities or functionings fall below minimum acceptable standards. It is quite possible, hence, for one to be capability-poor but not income-poor.[2]

The third way of looking at poverty is to see it as a relationship between one person and another. We shall call this the social deprivation approach. Income and capabilities no doubt are relevant – they are 'intermediating' factors – but the essence of poverty according to this approach lies in relations among people. The poor are those who are socially deprived; they are people whose incomes, capabilities or other characteristics are unacceptably distant from the norms of their community or reference group. To be poor is to fall below the minimum accepted standards of one's society, to live in shame, to be indecent, to be unable to participate fully in the life of the community. Poverty here is a social construct which has little to do with physiological requirements and the like (minimum calories, basic needs or minimum incomes) or with capabilities (longevity, mobility, literacy, numeracy and the like). It is quite possible that a person could be regarded by her community as poor – and would regard herself as poor – even though she were not income-poor or capability-poor. She would be poor because relative to other individuals her capabilities or income are low.

These three approaches to the definition of poverty are not exclusive. Countries may use one approach in one context and a different approach in another, or a combination of approaches. Indeed, this is exactly what happens in Mongolia, where all three approaches can be found side-by-side. When estimating the extent of poverty nationwide, an income-poverty approach is used. When designing programmes to alleviate poverty, implicitly a capabilities approach has been used, those in poverty being identified as members of six so-called vulnerable groups.[3] And when local officials have to decide how to spend the meagre funds they have to alleviate poverty, the social-deprivation approach has been used.[4]

It usually is taken for granted that poverty is undesirable and that public policy should have as one of its objectives the alleviation of poverty or, better still, its elimination. Nonetheless, it is important to consider the purpose of poverty alleviation, the reasons why a reduction in poverty is regarded as a matter of high priority. Four reasons, we think, can be identified; although they overlap, they are distinct.

First, and most obvious, the purpose of poverty alleviation is to *raise the well-being* of those who are materially disadvantaged. Second, the purpose is to *increase the capabilities* of those whose basic capabilities fail to reach the minimally acceptable levels. This would include measures, for example, to avoid damage to the intellects of children arising from severe malnutrition in infancy. A third purpose is to *promote economic development* by increasing human capital formation, i.e. by investing in people in order to raise the productivity of their labour. Finally, the purpose of poverty alleviation is to *increase freedom* in the positive sense of enabling people to lead a life of their choice, as well as in the negative sense of enabling people to be free, for example, of hunger. Conversely, if 'free' markets result in hunger for some people, that is a loss of freedom (namely 'freedom from hunger') for them, as well as a loss of well-being.

Thus just as there are several definitions of poverty, so too there are several reasons why the reduction or elimination of poverty could be, and in our view should be, a major objective of policy.

THE EXTENT OF POVERTY

The most widely-used measure of poverty is based on what we have called the income-poverty approach. Estimates in Mongolia of the number of people below the poverty-line or of the numbers who do not achieve the minimum living level use broadly similar procedures to those adopted in other countries. The income-poverty approach, however, is not quite as straightforward as it sometimes appears and it is worth considering briefly the cluster of related concepts that have been used:

(i) Household sample surveys have been used to construct poverty-lines centred on a minimum *per capita expenditure*. This of course raises the general problem, common to several of the concepts listed below, of how best to value own consumption. In a live-stock-based economy, for example, milk and meat may seldom be purchased but instead be self-provisioned.

(ii) Household surveys also have been used to construct poverty-lines centred on a minimum *per capita income*. Income and expenditure are not, of course, the same thing and in some circumstances it may be possible, say, for expenditure by poor households to exceed their income. This could occur, for example, if the poor go into debt in order to maintain consumption, or if they sell some of their assets. Moreover, there are various ways to define or measure income, and estimates of poverty may be quite sensitive to the definition of income used in the survey. Thus estimates of expenditure-poverty and various concepts of income-poverty may not coincide.

(iii) In some cases it might be feasible and more useful to define poverty not in terms of some minimum income or expenditure but in terms of the ownership of assets. Again in livestock communities, for example, one could define poverty as a minimum holding of *per capita assets*, expressed perhaps in sheep equivalents.[5] Especially where monetary expenditure is low and most income is self-provisioned, assets may be a better indicator of prosperity and poverty than other more conventional measures.

(iv) Attempts have sometimes been made to adjust for the age composition of households by taking into account the fact that the minimum requirements of children are less than those of adults. The conversion factor of children into adults is pretty arbitrary but perhaps it is no less arbitrary than the implicit conversion factor of 1:1 that is used when the minima are expressed in per capita terms. Where adjustments for age are made, the poverty line is centred on a minimum expenditure (or income or assets) *per adult equivalent*. Here again, estimates of poverty based on per capita calculations might not coincide exactly with estimates based on adult equivalent calculations.

(v) Yet another variant of the income-poverty approach is to centre estimates on a minimum *per capita food expenditure.* The implicit assumption here, as mentioned above, is that food is in some sense more 'basic' than other needs, e.g. the need for shelter, fuel or clothing, and should therefore be the defining characteristic of poverty. The overlap between households which are income-poor and food-expenditure-poor might not be high.

(vi) Lastly, many analysts regard poverty as rooted in a physiological phenomenon, namely, malnutrition. They therefore construct poverty-lines centred on a minimum *per capita calorie consumption.* Notice, however, that there may be only a weak correspondence between levels of food expenditure and levels of calorie consumption. If households raise the quality of their diet or increase the variety of foods consumed as incomes rise, there might not be any association between changes in income and changes in the number of calories consumed.

We thus have six slightly different concepts each consistent with the income-poverty approach, yet each likely to result in a different estimate of who is poor, and in the number of poor. None of the six is unambiguously superior to the others. The alternative estimates simply illustrate the point that there are several dimensions to poverty.

The official estimates in Mongolia indicate that poverty increased at a truly phenomenal rate during the first three years of the transition. In 1989 there was zero income-poverty: the central government, state enterprises and rural cooperatives (*negdels*) between them ensured that everyone satisfied their basic needs and had access to the full range of public services. By late 1992 the proportion of the population in poverty was 17 per cent. It rose further to 23 per cent in June 1993 and increased fractionally again to 23.6 per cent in October 1993. In March 1994 it was 26.5 per cent. The accuracy of these figures, however, is subject to doubt.

First, separate figures for the minimum living standard income (or poverty-line) are set for rural and urban areas, with the rural standard usually being significantly lower than the urban. Since the rural poverty-line includes an adjustment for non-monetised transactions, it is not obvious why the poverty-lines should differ markedly, especially since the availability of many goods is more restricted in rural areas and the prices of some goods (e.g. rice, pipe tobacco, electricity, water) are higher.[6] In addition, the price range of products in rural areas is exceptionally wide and hence it is unclear that it is possible to construct a single poverty-line applicable to all rural communities in Mongolia.

Second, the ratio of the rural to the urban poverty-line varies considerably and inexplicably from one period to another. For instance in December 1992 the rural minimum living standard income was said to be 75.8 per cent of the urban standard whereas six months later, in June 1993, the rural standard was only 65.8 per cent of the urban. By December 1993 the rural standard had risen to 90.6 per cent of the urban.

The enormous difference that often occurs in the nominal value of poverty-lines in rural and urban areas suggests that the standards applied in the two locations are inconsistent.[7] That is, two persons with identical real standards of living would be classified differently depending on where they happen to live. Furthermore, if someone just above the rural minimum living standard were to migrate to the city and receive an income just below the urban minimum living standard, the number of people recorded as living in poverty would rise. Indeed the difference in standards in June 1993 implies that a migrant from the countryside to the city who increases her nominal income by 50 per cent could nonetheless be recorded as having moved from rural non-poverty to urban poverty.

Third, the poverty-lines are revised every few months (or roughly twice a year) to take inflation into account, but it appears that the upward adjustment in the poverty-lines does not fully reflect the rise in prices. That is, the poverty-line, in real terms, seems to have fallen over time and hence one cannot compare changes in the proportion of the population in poverty from one period to the next. Consider again the changes between December 1992 and June 1993. Inflation for the whole of 1993 was 183 per cent; during the first six months it was 104.2 per cent. Yet the urban poverty-line in that six-month period was raised only 59.6 per cent and the rural poverty-line even less, namely, 38.7 per cent.

It seems likely therefore that the estimates of poverty contain serious biases. Poverty in the rural areas probably is underestimated relative to the urban areas. And the number of people in poverty (in both rural and urban areas) is probably increasingly understated with the passage of time. 'True' poverty in March 1994 probably was much higher than the official figures reported in Table 2.1.

Moreover the poverty-line itself is exceedingly ungenerous.[8] Gross national product per capita in 1993 was roughly $265 a year. The urban poverty-line in June of that year was about $49.20 a year, or less than 19 per cent of average incomes. The rural poverty-line was about $32.40 or just over 12 per cent of per capita GNP. The 'very poor' in

TABLE 2.1   Official estimates of poverty, March 1994

	Number of poor people	*Percentage of the population*
Poor	449 859	20.3
Very poor	137 423	6.2
Total	587 282	26.5

Table 2.1 comprise people with an income of less than 40 per cent of the minimum living standard. In the urban areas this implies an income of less than $20 a year and in the rural areas an income of less than $13. Not surprisingly, there are very few such people, although in some rural districts (*sums*) the 'very poor' exceed the merely 'poor'.

SAMPLING METHODOLOGY

The sampling procedures used to estimate the extent of income poverty are somewhat idiosyncratic and it is uncertain that the household income and expenditures survey generates accurate estimates of incomes of the population as a whole. Poverty estimates were first produced in 1990, based on a sample size of only 1250 households. The size of sample was enlarged to 1850 in 1993 but for budgetary reasons it is expected to contract by 20 per cent or more in future. There is some danger therefore that the sample size, even if properly constructed, will be too small to draw meaningful results.

The sample consists of panel data that is both stratified and purposeful (or non-random). The 1850 households are first divided in two: 54 per cent (999 households) are assigned to the urban areas and 46 per cent (851 households) to the rural. In the rural areas all *aimags* (provinces) are included, each *aimag* having a sample size of 70 households on average. The number of observations in each *aimag* evidently is too small for meaningful inferences to be drawn about the extent of poverty at the provincial level. Within each *aimag* one region (*sum*) is purposefully selected to represent the *aimag* as a whole. Every household in the selected *sum* is then interviewed and households are ranked by income. Thirty households are then selected for intensive study, the selection being based on a three-fold stratification. A similar procedure is followed in the *aimag* centre: one district is selected as representative of the town as a whole, all households are interviewed and ranked and 40 households are selected for detailed study.

Comparable methods are used to obtain estimates of household income and expenditure in the urban areas. In both rural and urban areas the selected households are interviewed every month throughout the year. Moreover, the same households are selected for study from one year to the next, a household being replaced only if for some reason it decides to drop out. The published data on poverty therefore are based on panel studies and do not reflect a reliable cross-section of the population. It is uncertain how the results are biased by using panel data, but it is likely that estimates of poverty are understated since newly-formed households (which presumably have lower incomes than average) are not introduced into the sample frame in a systematic way.

The panel data, if they were published, would be exceptionally interesting, since they would enable researchers to trace the effects of transition policies on individual households. This would greatly enrich our understanding of how economic processes unleashed during the shift from a planned to a market-guided economy operate and it would make it easier to design appropriate policies to combat poverty. Thus we are not suggesting that the panel studies be discontinued; we recommend instead that they be improved to be more representative and that the data be made generally available. In addition to the panel data, however, there is great need for a reliable household income and expenditure survey based on a randomly-selected cross-section of households. Only with such data will it be possible to estimate accurately the extent and depth of poverty. South Korea, India, Pakistan and Bangladesh have much experience in designing and implementing nationwide sample surveys and the Government should consider asking UNDP to provide technical assistance in survey techniques, possibly obtaining a specialist from one of these four countries.

THE POVERTY-LINE

The poverty-line in Mongolia is intended to represent a minimum standard of living that enables a person to satisfy her basic needs. Eight items or clusters of items are taken into account – namely, food, clothing, shelter, heating, household utensils, medical supplies, communication and cultural items (books, etc.) for children of school age. Norms are established for each and the minimum cost of reaching the norms is calculated using market prices. In the case of food, for example, the norm is 70 per cent of the recommended calorie intake (roughly 2000 kcal per day) and it is assumed, for instance, that half the meat consists of animal intestines and 70 per cent of the flour is second-grade. The minimum living standard is thus a hypothetical budget, i.e. the amount of money that in principle would be needed to reach the preset norms. There can be no presumption that individuals with a poverty-line income – 3200 tugriks in urban areas and 2900 tugriks in rural areas in December 1993 – actually would choose to spend their income in the ways postulated.[9] In other words, since the poverty-line does not reflect actual behaviour of households but only theoretical behaviour, there is no guarantee that those living on or just above the poverty line would satisfy their basic needs.

The hypothetical budget calculations are made separately for rural and urban areas. Within each area, different poverty-lines are calculated for individual household members, taking into account differences in age and sex. The exercise is thus rather elaborate and abstract. It would be much better in our view to base estimates of the minimum living standard on observed behaviour rather than rely on theoretical models of household budgets. After all, the purpose, presumably, of the poverty-line calculation is to enable estimates to be made of how many people in practice fail to meet their basic needs. The poverty-line as presently calculated enables no such estimate to be made. At best it indicates the number of people who could not meet their basic needs even if they spent their income strictly in accordance with the assumptions of a planner in the Ministry of Population Policy and Labour (MPPL) and the State Statistical Office (SSO).

The administrative arrangements for calculating and periodically revising the poverty-line appear to be rather cumbersome. The MPPL sets the norms and the SSO makes the hypothetical budget calculations. The final determination of the minimum living-level, however, is made by the Cabinet. This inevitably creates a suspicion, which may be completely unjustified, that political considerations enter into the choice of the poverty-line. To avoid this suspicion, it would be better not to involve senior politicians in the twice-yearly re-estimation of the minimum living standard.

It would also help to allay suspicions if information on the national income and expenditures survey and the results of poverty estimates were more readily available to the public. At present, for example, the government releases information only on the number of persons who fall below the poverty-line and on the number whose income is less than 40 per cent of the minimum living standard. Thus there are no estimates of the distribution of income in the country as a whole. We are not even told what is the mean income of the poor and hence it is impossible to estimate how much the average income of the poor would have to rise in order to eliminate income poverty. Better still, of course, would be information on the distribution of income among those classified as poor. This would make it possible to determine whether large numbers of poor people are very close to the poverty-line, or alternatively, whether most poor people are some distance away from the poverty threshold. All of this information could be readily obtained from the results of the household survey and it is cause for regret that the data are not more fully analysed.

FROM INCOME POVERTY TO CAPABILITY POVERTY

Given the weaknesses in the measurement of income poverty in Mongolia, it is useful, quite apart from its conceptual advantages, to have an alternative approach which focuses on capabilities. The government has done this by identifying six 'vulnerable groups' and these have been singled out for special attention. The phrase 'vulnerable groups' can be interpreted in several ways, but perhaps it is most natural to interpret it to mean that certain people are exposed to exceptional risks that others do not normally face, risks that can plunge an individual or household into poverty. These risks or vulnerabilities might be associated with the life cycle (such as the vulnerabilities faced by the aged), or with family structures which provide little support in emergencies (such as female-headed households) or with high fluctuations in incomes and assets which can threaten food security (such as can occur among herders with a low value of (animal) assets per member of the household). Some members of vulnerable groups may face transient or temporary spells of poverty whereas others may face chronic poverty. And of course some individuals who are not members of a vulnerable group might nonetheless face serious risks (such as the risk of a prolonged illness).

The vulnerable groups that have been identified in Mongolia, and the members of which are therefore eligible for poverty relief, are (i) children who have lost one or both parents; (ii) disabled persons; (iii) the elderly; (iv) female-headed households; (v) households with many children, and hence a high dependency ratio and (vi) the unemployed. Conspicuously missing from this list are herders with low incomes and assets, a group that faces exceptional climatic and other risks and is regarded by many as the largest single group of poor people. Of course risk as such would not matter terribly if insurance markets were well developed, but neither in Mongolia nor in other countries do insurance markets cover all contingencies. Virtually everywhere the government is the 'insurer of last resort', whether it be in the United States (where the government recently has had to come to the aid of people affected by a hurricane in Florida, floods in the Middle West and an earthquake in California) or in developing countries where the consequences of unforeseen unfavourable events can be particularly devastating.

Risk is not the whole story, however. Some of the groups classified as vulnerable really suffer from impaired capabilities and it is this that establishes their claim on public resources allocated to the alleviation of poverty. The elderly, for example, as Amartya Sen points out, suffer from an 'income-earning handicap' combined with an 'income-using handicap'. They have a 'harder time in being free from disease, in leading a healthy life, in achieving mobility, in taking part in the life of the community, in seeing friends, and so on'.[10] They may, in some cases, have an income which puts them above the poverty-line, and hence they would not be classified as income-poor, but their capabilities may be so reduced that they are regarded as capability-poor. The essential point is that the ability of people to convert calories, basic needs or income into capabilities varies enormously depending on circumstances and it is in principle correct that Mongolia should adopt a capabilities approach in trying to identify the poor.

It is also right, we think, that the funds allocated to alleviating capability poverty should be administered by local government and that local government should be given considerable discretion in how best to spend the money. The problem is that the amounts allocated to the so-called Social Assistance Fund are derisory, less than $1 per person per year for each person below the poverty-line.[11] In Ulaanbaatar, where a third of the funds have been allocated, the programme is managed by a local official in an urban neighbourhood (*horoo*) containing roughly 1500 households. The official is advised by a volunteer committee of local citizens who know the people in their neighbourhood and thus are in a position to make reasonable assessments of need. A similar model, adapted to rural conditions, is also used in the provinces and the *sums*. This management model for the relief of capability poverty is promising: it is flexible, highly decentralised and based on community participation. The next step is to enlarge the fund so that it can have a significant impact.

It must be recognised, however, that the identification of groups with common disadvantageous characteristics (the elderly, the unemployed, etc.)

has limitations. The great merit of selecting 'vulnerable groups' for special attention is that specific programmes can be designed which target the intended beneficiaries: pensions for the elderly, public works projects for the unemployed, and so on. The disadvantages are, first, that some members of vulnerable groups may not in fact be poor and, second, some poor people may not belong to a vulnerable group. In the latter case, some people living in poverty, and therefore deserving public support, may be excluded unintentionally from official schemes intended to alleviate hardship. What is needed in such cases is an approach to poverty-alleviation that focuses on individuals rather than on groups which have some particular feature in common. The social deprivation approach allows one to do this.

SOCIAL DEPRIVATION AND COMMUNITY PARTICIPATION

In Mongolia it is the responsibility of local government officials to identify the poor and deliver relief. This is a very sensible arrangement since communications between Ulaanbaatar and provincial capitals is difficult and local conditions among the small, scattered and isolated rural communities can vary enormously. One consequence of this is that two persons in similar circumstances, i.e. with the same real income and the same basic capabilities, might be regarded differently depending upon the general conditions in the communities in which they reside. That is, one person may be poor in the sense of being socially deprived compared to the others in her reference group while the other may not be poor, since her situation is not markedly inferior to that of others in her community.

In general, those identified by local officials as living in poverty tend to belong to one of the vulnerable groups or to have an income below the poverty-line, or both. Moreover, those granted assistance tend to be the very poorest of the poor, i.e. those with the lowest real incomes. It is noteworthy, however, that when asked in a survey to define poverty, the 25 *sum* governors consulted identified the poor as 'one who possesses few or no animals, does not have relatives who are able to look after him, has few clothes, no steady income of his own and is unable to find work'.[12]

This definition of poverty begins with assets ('few or no animals'), refers to social position ('does not have relatives'), considers basic needs ('has few clothes'), takes the variability of income into account and concludes with a reference to a vulnerable group ('is unable to find work'). This definition, in other words, is much richer, more comprehensive, more sensitive to variations in local conditions than the rather blunt instruments of the poverty-line and vulnerable groups. Poverty-lines and the designation of vulnerable groups should be used in Mongolia as a framework to guide local policy decisions. In remote, tightly-knit rural communities there should be little difficulty identifying the poor and determining what type of assistance is required or would be most useful. The 25 *sum* governors surveyed readily agreed that 'poverty was very easy to spot due to the relatively small number of people in their areas and because of those people all knowing each other well'.[13]

Local officials, especially those at the *sum* level, may not be well-informed about conditions in regions other than their own, but they are better-informed than anyone else about conditions in their locality. There is thus a strong case for giving local government the responsibility for identifying the poor and implementing policies to alleviate poverty. The resources, however, given the weak revenue base of the provinces, must be provided by the central government. This, too, is appropriate since it is the central government that is in the best position to compare the relative needs of the different provinces and allocate funds among the provinces in accordance with their relative needs.

We thus recommend that the social-deprivation approach to poverty be used at the local level to identify the poor and devise effective local remedies while the income-poverty and capabilities approaches be used to create a national policy framework. Ultimately, it is individuals who are poor in relation to the norms of those who live in their particular community, that is, their neighbours, friends and fellow workers. Poverty, in this sense, always is local, whereas policy is national.

SUMMARY AND CONCLUSIONS

Poverty in Mongolia has become a serious problem and a major policy issue. This is true whether poverty is defined as insufficient income, as a failure to enjoy basic capabilities or as social deprivation. These three different conceptions of the nature of the poverty problem produce broadly similar results as regards orders of magnitude and the kinds of individuals affected, but they are distinct and have different implications for policy.

Official estimates of the number of poor are based on a nationwide household income and expenditure survey and a poverty-line (or minimum living-standard income) which, in turn, is based on a set of minimum basic needs. The methodology of the household surveys suffers from several weaknesses. While the sample size is large enough for a national estimate of the incidence of poverty, it is much too small to produce accurate estimates of poverty at the provincial level. The information obtained from the survey consists of panel data and not a genuine cross-section of the population. This biases the results and almost certainly leads to an underestimation of the number of poor people. The data are not drawn from a random sample but from a stratified sample with purposive observations at each stage of sampling, This, too, introduces a bias to the results that may also lead to an underestimation of the extent of poverty.

The poverty-line itself raises several questions. The norms (or minimum needs) are exceedingly low. The minimum income needed to achieve the norms is based on a hypothetical budget which severely constrains the way people spend their total income; it would be better, we think, to derive the minimum required income from observations of how people actually spend their incomes. Both the low norms and the hypothetical budget tend to reduce the estimates of poverty compared to alternative procedures.

Although on the surface it appears to be reasonable to calculate separate poverty-lines for the urban and rural areas, the difference in the two poverty-lines strains credibility. The problem is accentuated by the enormous differences within the rural areas and raises the question whether it makes sense to attempt to construct a single poverty-line applicable to the diverse conditions in rural Mongolia.

Finally, it appears that the real value of the minimum living standard income has fallen over time, i.e. the poverty-line appears not to have been adjusted to take inflation fully into account. There are reasons to believe therefore that rural poverty is understated relative to urban poverty and that total poverty has been increasingly understated over time relative to the basic-needs norms.

The identification of six vulnerable groups – which corresponds roughly to what we have called capability poverty – is a partial corrective to the income-poverty approach. High risks faced by certain groups undoubtedly increase the likelihood that at some point in their life – possibly in connection with a life-cycle-event – many and perhaps most of the members of a particular group will fall into poverty. Insofar as risk is the criterion for determining vulnerability, however, it is rather odd that herders with low per capita holdings of animal assets are not listed as one of the vulnerable groups. In the absence of a full array of insurance markets, in Mongolia and elsewhere, the government must act as the insurer of last resort, and this role is likely to be of special importance for vulnerable herders.

Some other vulnerable groups, in contrast, suffer not from unusually high risks but from impaired capabilities. The identification of such vulnerable groups is useful because it provides an incentive to government to design policies and programmes aimed at specific targets. In the final analysis, however, poverty is a local phenomenon that affects people as individuals or as household units. Particularly in Mongolian conditions, poverty-alleviation programmes, to be successful, will have to reflect local conditions and be implemented locally.

What, then, should be done?

Mongolia faces a poverty emergency. Conditions are bad and they are getting worse. The seriousness of the situation is partly disguised by the very even distribution of income that existed before the transition began. People in 1989 were well-housed and well-clothed and consequently they have been able to respond to falling incomes in part by not repairing their *gers* (felt tents or yurts) or replacing their clothing. In effect, families have been consuming part of their household capital. This process, however, cannot continue much longer. Boots will wear out, clothing will become rags, tent canvases will have become so patched they cannot be repaired further. Already in some areas layers of paper are used instead of felt for insulation. Poverty, now almost invisible to outsiders, soon will become ugly, and in the extreme winter climate of Mongolia, dangerous as well.

There is an urgent need to create an emergency Growth, Employment and Poverty Alleviation Fund from either domestic or external resources. The initial size of the fund should be US$21 million, with a notional allocation of $1 million to each of the 18 *aimags* or provinces and $1 million to each of the three cities of Choir, Darkhan and Erdenet.[14] The purposes of the fund would be the following:

(i) to finance small local capital projects to alleviate bottlenecks in infrastructure (power and small diesel generators, roads and road vehicles, communications);

(ii) to finance small and medium local public works programmes, the repair, renovation and construction of public buildings, including clinics and schools (e.g. adapting school buildings for the use of traditional and cheaper forms of heating) and any other labour-intensive investment projects likely to promote growth;

(iii) to promote small-scale production activities, including small-scale enterprises, herders, local cooperatives, etc. This would include providing finance capital in the form of loans at positive real rates of interest for purchasing equipment and supplies, re-stocking herds, purchasing agricultural machinery, transport equipment and equipment needed to process livestock products. The loans would be administered through a variety of mechanisms, depending on local circumstances, including local government, local commercial banks, non-bank financial institutions and other more innovative mechanisms (such as revolving funds, credit circles), where these can be established quickly. Promotion under this heading could also include provision of vocational training, information, legal and technical advice concerning marketing and accounting methods, possibly provided by newly-established Local Enterprise Promotion Centres; and

(iv) to eliminate the worst forms of poverty through direct transfers (in cash or kind as appropriate) to those in greatest need, including assistance to children from poor families to attend school.

The proposal, thus, is to create a comprehensive or omnibus fund to address local poverty problems within the framework of Mongolia's highly-decentralised system of governance. Seen from the centre (or from the office of a donor agency) the proposal could be criticised for seeking a 'one shot' solution; seen from the provinces (or by those seeking tailor-made solutions to their specific problems) the proposal could be criticised for adopting a 'shotgun' solution. In fact it is neither; it is a flexible tool which can be used to address diverse situations in geographically remote and highly differentiated regions.

The fund would be administered by the Ministry of Population Policy and Labour under the supervision of the National Council for Poverty Alleviation. The Ministry would set guidelines, possibly including a ceiling on the proportion of funds that could be distributed as transfers, but the choice of projects for finance and responsibility for implementation would lie with the governors of each province. The governor, in turn, would be advised by a local council made up of organisations representing local interest groups. The programme, thus, would be highly decentralised, would permit local experimentation in strategy and tactics, would provide for local participation of all relevant groups and would permit differences in local conditions to be reflected in expenditure allocations among the wide range of eligible activities.

The Ministry would be responsible for monitoring results in the *aimags* and communicating the lessons learned from the competing approaches. In order to provide a strong incentive to the 18 provincial governments to design their strategy carefully and to implement projects and programmes efficiently, the initial allocation to each *aimag* should only be \$0.5 million; the remaining half of the fund would be allocated in a second round to those *aimags* that demonstrate their ability to use funds effectively. Mongolia is blessed with an excellent structure of local government and with local officials who are competent and who have a strong commitment to serving their people. The injection of competition among local governments for the exceedingly scarce funds for poverty alleviation is intended to ensure that the funds make the largest possible contribution to reducing poverty; it is not intended to be a vote of no confidence in local government; quite the contrary, the awarding of a high degree of discretion to local government reflects our belief that local administration should take the lead in reducing poverty.[15]

If the emergency Growth, Employment and Poverty Alleviation Fund proves to be a success, as we believe it will, it ought to be replenished and extended for several years. It is important, therefore, that, say, three-quarters through its first year of operations, the Ministry evaluates progress in the use of the fund, produces proposals for improvement and assesses future needs.

NOTES

1. Meghnad Desai, 'Income and Alternative Measures of Well-Being', in David G. Westendorff and Dharam Ghai (eds), *Monitoring Social Progress in the 1990s* (Aldershot: Avebury, 1993), p. 31.
2. On the capability approach to poverty see Amartya Sen, *Inequality Reexamined* (Cambridge: Harvard University Press, 1992), Ch. 7.
3. In some cases, as in the Social Assistance Fund, a combination of the income and capabilities approaches is used.
4. Quite apart from the conceptual superiority of the social-deprivation approach, it also has a practical superiority in that it permits local officials to use a wider range of information than is available from survey data in judging who is or is not poor.
5. Alternatively, in Mongolia one could convert animal assets into *bods*, the unit used in some nomadic communities, where 1 *bod* = $\frac{2}{3}$ camel or 1 horse or 1 cow or 7 sheep or 10 goats.

6. Research and Consultancy Centre of the Institute of Administration and Management Development, *A Survey of Rural Poverty*, Ulaanbaatar, December 1993, Table 3, p. 4 and Appendix Tables 1–4.
7. See Martin Ravaillion and Benu Bidami, 'How Robust Is a Poverty Profile?', *World Bank Economic Review*, Vol. 8, no. 1, January 1994.
8. There are reports in Ulaanbaatar of families living in *gers* having to spend the equivalent of 30 per cent of the poverty-line income on water alone, the water being hauled into the neighbourhood by truck.
9. The exchange rate is approximately US$1 = 400 tugriks.
10. Amartya Sen, op. cit., p. 113.
11. United Nations Development Programme, *Mongolia: Poverty Alleviation Strategy*, Background Paper, draft, December 1993. We have not been able to obtain estimates of the total number of capability-poor persons who belong to the six 'vulnerable groups'. We have therefore expressed the financial allocations in terms of dollars per head of the income-poor.
12. Research and Consultancy Centre of the Institute of Administrative and Management Development, op. cit., p. 1.
13. Ibid., p. 2.
14. Ulaanbaatar is excluded from the allocation from this fund because it already is the beneficiary of a US$3 million employment programme financed by the Asian Development Bank, and many other aid projects.
15. The question of the ability of local government to administer a development programme of the type envisaged is discussed in Chapter 10. Also discussed are national-level issues such as preparation and enforcement of guidelines and monitoring the use of funds. One should perhaps also note here that UNDP has initiated a Management Development Programme, one purpose of which is to strengthen administrative capacities at the local level.

3 Employment Promotion and the Social Safety-Net

Wouter von Ginneken

In Chapter 1 it was argued that there are three strategic tasks that must be completed successfully in order to effect the transition from a centrally planned to a market-guided economy. First, the level of aggregate demand must be reduced to reflect the productive capacity of the economy. Second, the composition of expenditure must shift in favour of human and physical investment in order to accelerate the growth of output and average incomes. Third, relative prices must be restructured in order to provide incentives to employ labour, use capital efficiently and exploit opportunities for profitable international trade.

In this chapter we focus on the third of these conditions, paying particular attention to the set of incentives affecting the employment of labour, the acquisition and use of skills, and the opportunities to create small-scale, labour-intensive private sector enterprises and activities. Although we shall concentrate on relative prices – and especially on the 'key' price of the real wage rate for unskilled labour – we shall also, where appropriate, comment on administrative controls that influence the pattern of employment and the degree of labour intensity in production.

Markets, relative prices and the structure of incentives influence allocative efficiency, the rate of growth, the distribution of income and the incidence of poverty. All of these evidently are important, but our concern is with poverty alleviation and hence efficiency, growth and income distribution will not be considered in their own right but only insofar as they have a significant impact on changes in the number of poor people and in the average incomes of those in poverty. For example, we are interested in obstacles to the emergence of a vibrant private sector not just because they reduce the aggregate rate of growth but above all because the creation of small-scale private-enterprise activities is an easy and rapid way to reduce unemployment, raise the productivity of labour and ameliorate poverty. We are interested in the allocation of bank credit and in real interest rates not because they determine whether finance capital is used efficiently but because they influence the pace of growth and the composition of output and hence the speed with which poverty is reduced. That is, our purpose is to examine how markets actually function in Mongolia, particularly labour markets, and to discover whether actual markets function in such a way as to aggravate or assuage poverty.

In this chapter we shall first address issues of employment and labour incomes in Mongolia, based on statistics that were designed not for our purposes but for the workings of a centrally planned economy. We shall then propose a strategy to increase the productive employment of labour and finally provide the outlines of a social safety-net for those who either are not able to work or cannot find work.

EMPLOYMENT AND UNEMPLOYMENT

The labour market undoubtedly is functioning poorly. Mongolia's employment situation has deteriorated rapidly since 1989. Unemployment has risen, particularly in the rural areas and among young people and women, and labour incomes have fallen, namely wages in the urban areas and income from livestock production in the rural areas.

Roughly half of Mongolia's population of 2.25 million is of working age, namely 1.1 million people. The labour force participation rate (LFPR) at the end of 1993 was 83.3 per cent (70 per cent for women and 97 per cent for men), which implies that about 900 000 Mongolians were either working or looking for a job. The Mongolian labour force is young: 59.6 per cent of those employed are under the age of 35. Because of rapid population growth in the past, fostered by a pro-natalist policy, the labour force is currently increasing by 3.4 per cent per year. Around 50 000 young job-seekers are entering the labour market each year.

The structure of employment has changed considerably during the transition. Mainly as a result of the privatisation of livestock, many people have attempted to obtain a livelihood by entering agriculture. In this sector about 40 000 new jobs were created between 1990 and 1993. On the other hand, employment in the public sector has dropped significantly. According to estimates of the Ministry of Population Policy and Labour (MPPL) employment in state enterprises dropped from 460 000 in 1991 to 350 000 in 1992, while employment in 'privatised' enterprises increased from 32 000 to 111 000. The administrative procedures used in collecting data on current employment makes it impossible to obtain accurate estimates of the number of self-employed, but rough estimates made by the MPPL indicate that the number of self-employed persons has risen from 22 000 to more than 76 000. In the public services significant declines were registered, as also occurred in the construction and transportation sectors. Another consequence of the crisis and the transition is a decline in employment opportunities for women (see Table 3.1). Between 1990 and 1992 the proportion of women in employment dropped from almost 49 per cent to 46 per cent. (The employment of women, particularly in the informal sector, is discussed further in Chapter 6.)

With labour supply outstripping employment opportunities, rising unemployment has been the inevitable outcome. Prior to the transition there was no unemployment in Mongolia and hence no poverty arising from the inability of able and willing workers to find a job and obtain a source of livelihood. There may have been disguised unemployment in the form of an excessive number of workers employed in state enterprises and in the rural collectives, and this had implications for microeconomic efficiency, but disguised or hidden unemployment did not result in poverty. That began to change, however, when the economic reforms were introduced. Registered unemployment stood at 71 900 at the end of 1993 or over 8 per cent of the labour force. Young first-time job-seekers, however, probably are underestimated by the employment services registration. In fact, if there were a proper labour force sample survey, total unemployment would probably be shown to be in the range of 90 000 to 110 000 (i.e. 10–12 per cent of the labour force). In addition there is fragmentary evidence of large numbers of workers who are temporarily laid off and not counted as unemployed.

Young people (up to 25 years old) are most likely to be without a job. They represent 55 per cent of the registered unemployed. About 30 per cent of all unemployed (about 23 000 people at the end of 1993) have higher education, special secondary education or a vocational training qualification. In fact, one out of five of the unemployed is a graduate of a vocational training centre. Also women are disproportionately affected: they are recorded, in January 1994, as accounting for 53.4 per cent of the unemployed, as compared to about 45 per cent of the labour force.

Perhaps surprisingly, unemployment does not appear to be a predominantly urban problem. Only 17.8 per cent of all registered unemployed live in Ulaanbaatar and in the three towns of Darkhan, Erdenet and Choir (compared to 32 per cent of the labour force). From the available data it is not clear whether the unemployed are therefore

TABLE 3.1   Employment by sector (in thousands) and by the proportion
who are women (in %), 1990–92

	1990		1991		1992	
	'000	%	'000	%	'000	%
Agriculture	256.1	45.3	270.9	44.0	290.7	44.8
Industry	131.6	48.3	132.2	49.2	133.9	47.9
Construction	66.1	36.2	49.4	36.6	41.5	38.1
Trade and supply	54.6	63.9	51.9	62.4	53.8	61.2
Transport and communications	57.7	28.1	52.2	29.7	50.2	27.9
Finance and insurance	3.9	66.7	4.4	61.4	5.0	58.0
Housing and domestic service	33.9	57.2	26.0	56.2	25.2	53.2
Science, education and culture	86.8	64.4	83.5	63.4	78.2	62.3
Public health	49.2	77.8	49.2	79.5	44.9	76.2
Public administration	32.1	31.8	29.3	31.7	29.7	29.6
Others*	11.6	76.8	40.8	41.2	52.9	37.8
TOTAL	783.6	48.9	789.8	47.4	806.0	46.2

* Most of those in this category probably are self-employed.

Source: Calculated from tabulations provided by the MPPL.

concentrated in the capital cities of the *aimags* or at the level of the
sums. If we assume that people working in livestock and agriculture
do not register as unemployed, and as we know that the unemployment rate in Ulaanbaatar is somewhere around 4–5 per cent, it follows
that average unemployment in the *aimag* capital cities and the *sum*
cities must range between 15 and 20 per cent. This has important implications for a poverty alleviation strategy, and strengthens the case
for an *aimag*-based Growth, Employment and Poverty Alleviation Fund
as discussed in Chapter 2.

WAGES AND OTHER LABOUR INCOMES

Real wage levels have been falling steadily over the last three years.
Whereas consumer prices rose by more than twenty times between
January 1991 and January 1994, average wages and salaries in 'state
budget organisations' (the public sector) increased by only eight times.
So public-sector workers experienced a loss of about 60 per cent of
their real salaries during those three years. The minimum-wage index

rose by 896 per cent during the same period and hence private formal sector workers on minimum wages may have lost slightly less purchasing power. In general, however, there has been a collapse in real wages since the transition began.

The rapid decline in real wages in the public as well as in the private formal sector has led to multi-jobbing and to an explosive growth of informal sector activities, particularly in Ulaanbaatar. Many public-sector workers try to supplement their wages by various trade and advisory activities, while some have left the formal (private) sector voluntarily in order to earn a higher living in the informal sector.[1] Given the currently high real interest rates, very few people borrow money to venture into manufacturing activities. Most are involved in trade, personal services or repair services. The reason why informal sector activities are most prevalent and remunerative in Ulaanbaatar probably has much to do with the relatively large amount of foreign exchange spent in Ulaanbaatar by the large and growing number of foreign personnel and aid projects. A smaller part of the demand may come from foreign investment, which since 1991 has created something like 5000 new jobs.

In the rural areas incomes have fallen because of unfavourable terms of trade for livestock and livestock products, as compared to the prices paid for the consumer goods herders buy (such as sugar, flour, tea and textiles).[2] As the liberalisation of farm-gate prices for livestock and livestock products was delayed until 1993, and other prices were liberalised in 1991 and before, livestock producers (both individual herders and livestock companies) faced a continuously worsening economic climate in the early 1990s. Meat-rationing was discontinued in August 1993, but local town governments still try to control prices for meat sold through 'official' marketing channels.

The employment and income picture presented above is based on statistics using concepts and methodologies that were designed for the workings of a centrally planned economy. In Chapter 2 we commented on the quality of the Family Budget Survey. In this chapter we note that in Mongolia concepts such as unemployment and the economically active labour force and the way industries are classified do not conform to internationally accepted standards. In addition, Mongolia's statistics are mainly obtained by administrative methods, rather than obtained directly at the household or enterprise level. As a result, there is no integrated system of employment and income statistics, and this hinders the development of policies for employment and poverty alleviation.

AN EMPLOYMENT STRATEGY

Mongolia's principal natural wealth lies in the rural areas, partly in minerals but mostly in its cattle, camels, sheep and goats, providing skins and wool for which there is a strong international demand. So the first challenge for a strategy towards employment-creation and poverty-alleviation is to improve the productive employment of the herders and all those who are involved in the marketing and processing of livestock and livestock products. The foreign exchange earned by exporting these basic products is particularly valuable since it will make it possible to import the inputs required by the private sector in industry and services.

Of course, there is some foreign investment, but as discussed in Chapter 11, this will come in large quantities only when Mongolia has managed to develop a self-sustaining and growing economy. Another factor that masks the basic economic reality of a severe foreign exchange constraint is the large inflow – welcome as it is – of foreign exchange from international aid. Foreign aid to Mongolia is now abundant, compared with that to most other developing countries, but that could change very quickly in future.

The promotion of productive and remunerative employment in the urban areas is the second great challenge for an employment-oriented policy of poverty alleviation. The development of the private sector – cooperatives as well as formal and informal sector enterprises – plays a central part here. Methods to improve productivity in the public sector also are important but will not be discussed as they do not have a direct impact on poverty alleviation. The third challenge is the development of human capital, as discussed at some length in Chapters 4 and 5. In this chapter we shall discuss a few aspects of training and measures to improve the functioning of the labour market. And finally, the fourth challenge is to provide a social safety-net for those who either are not able to work or cannot find work. Here we shall discuss labour-intensive public works and the Social Assistance Fund.

(i) Rural Employment Promotion

Mongolia missed opportunities to increase rural employment during the period of central planning. Agricultural productivity was stagnant for decades because of policies which placed emphasis on rapid capital-intensive industrialisation and urbanisation.[3] This inherited situation has now created a strong opportunity for exploiting both output and employment growth through the correction of the urban bias of the past and the promotion of agricultural growth. However, these opportunities have so far only been partially seized. The almost total privatisation of livestock collectives and state farms has contributed to a rise in labour absorption into agriculture, especially in the livestock sector. These gains have, however, remained modest since, as noted earlier, procurement prices have only been partly liberalised and significant controls still are maintained over agricultural marketing and distribution. In addition, the government still controls the export of live animals and meat and bans the export of cashmere; it attempts, not always successfully, to force livestock producers in many parts of Mongolia to sell livestock and livestock products to government agencies.

The rural poor are livestock-poor households. They are on average younger, have higher dependency ratios and less herding experience than more wealthy households. Poor households have smaller herds, a less diverse herd structure and fewer large stock for herding (horses) and transport (camels). Households headed by women are more likely to be poor.

As discussed in Chapter 7, a two-pronged approach is required to address the problems of the rural poor. The aim should be, first, to develop conditions for the growth of the extensive sector generally (market development, infrastructure, service delivery in health and other services) and, second, to develop policies which target the poorest households specifically (credit schemes, welfare transfers to guarantee access to fodder, medicines, livestock or draught animals).

An initial step that would improve the production potential of marginal producers would involve the development of credit schemes to enable the poorest households to gain access to more livestock or certain types of livestock such as draught animals. At the same time it will be necessary to provide safety-nets for poor households through a variety of transfers in cash or in kind (food, clothing, fuel, fodder).

In addition, the poor should be helped to exploit market opportunities and improve incomes through improved prices and increased sales of livestock products. Their ability to do so may depend on their gaining access to credit, transport and simple technology for local processing. Particular attention should be paid to the needs of poor rural women and female-headed rural households.

An important consideration is the effectiveness of existing local institutions. Rural institutions play an important part in supporting poor and vulnerable households but they cannot by themselves increase the productive potential and well-being of the poorest; they can at best, given their inadequate resources, only prevent further impoverishment in the short term. However, some of these traditional institutions have experience in managing risk and spreading risk for those asset-poor households engaged in livestock herding. It may be possible to build on these existing forms of cooperation among households, e.g. by assisting them to take on credit risks and other potential development roles.

(ii) Promoting Non-Farm Employment

There is considerable potential for employment generation through the promotion of rural small industries based on the processing of agricultural products and the development of rural non-farm activities in general. So far, small enterprise and cooperative promotion programmes have been largely confined to urban centres, and the time has come to reverse this trend. Women, in particular, may be able to build on their experience and existing skills and take the lead in creating small rural enterprises. (This is discussed at length in Chapter 6.)

Herder and other rural households are well-placed to manufacture simple household items such as clothes and saddles, to process livestock products such as washing wool, processing milk, producing hard cheese, tanning leather, and even creating marketing enterprises. Currently, most of the processing of livestock products (wool, leather, meat, etc.) takes place either in Ulaanbaatar or, in the case of meat products, in Darkhan and Choybalsan. With decreasing reliance on central procurement, and central planning in general, there will be increasing opportunities for rural agriculture-based industry at the *sum* and *aimag* levels. As a complement to these activities there will be a greater need for storage facilities, market-places and roads and tracks connecting households, *sum* centres and *aimag* centres.

(iii) Large Private Sector Enterprises

As part of the transition to a market economy Mongolia decided at the beginning of the 1990s to privatise most of the economy. In 1991 restrictions on the private ownership of livestock were eliminated, and an extremely ambitious privatisation programme was launched. While before 1991 virtually all production took place in the public or collective sectors, in 1992 the share of the private sector was estimated to be 43 per cent for industry, 98 per cent for agriculture and 62 per cent overall.

In spite of the formal privatisation of public enterprises, management is still very much under the control of the government, which often holds more than 50 per cent of the shares. Where government has a minority of shares the workers and management between them often have more than 50 per cent and in such circumstances they tend not to be responsive to the interests of a diffuse group of residual shareholders. The Ministry of Trade and Industry still often performs the planning and command role of the past. In many cases the government continues to carry the losses of privatised enterprises and to provide directed credit subsidies. As a result, inflation is accelerated and the rest of the private sector encounters severe difficulties in obtaining working capital through the banking system.

Bankruptcy laws are not applied. Subsidisation cannot continue at present levels, but neither is it possible just to close down unprofitable enterprises: not only because of the employment implications but also because many of these national industries may prove to be commercially viable once stabilisation is achieved. The public utilities also are loss-making, because of inefficiency and the political difficulty of increasing prices in a context of falling real wages. The large state and privatised enterprises should therefore be given a little time to restructure and to see whether they can survive after being exposed to competition from foreign and other national enterprises. Any subsidies offered should be transparent and financed out of tax revenues.

Under the Law on Foreign Investment, foreign enterprises are granted tax holidays for five years. Since its adoption in 1991, some 330 foreign enterprises have been established in Mongolia. Most of them are in light manufacturing, retail trade and hotels. In the 130 units established in Ulaanbaatar 5000 new jobs have been created. One example of a successful company is the Temuujin Mench garment factory – a Canadian-Mongolian joint venture – that employs 3000 women and exports all its output to the United States. One obstacle to the emergence of other such enterprises is the difficulty in obtaining permits.

(iv) Small Enterprises and Cooperatives

The emphasis in industry and in the service sectors should in future shift away from large companies and be placed on the development of small and medium enterprises, concentrating initially on activities that meet demands of the domestic market and that are likely to create considerable amounts of employment. Some of these enterprises ultimately could enter the export market after they have achieved success supplying the domestic market. The service sector is already showing signs of generating employment in areas such as tourism, external and internal trade, business and professional services, and distribution. Some export-oriented industries such as garments and small import-substituting consumer goods industries have also begun to grow. In addition, there is potential for the development of activities such as construction, the production of construction materials such as bricks, cement and wood as well as the provision of electrical and plumbing services.

Enterprises in Mongolia, however, still face a number of obstacles which can be grouped into four categories.[4] First, some of the obstacles arise from the general environment and include such things as a high inflation rate; limited supply of credit and foreign exchange; an underdeveloped and unstable policy and legal environment; inadequate infrastructure; lack of adequate premises; and a generally hostile perception of small business by government. Second, the financial system is underdeveloped and hence small enterprises have difficulties obtaining credit and capital. Because of conflicting government regulations, small and medium enterprises often prefer to operate outside the banking system. Third, market constraints arise from the small size of the domestic market as well as from the inaccessibility of export markets due to poor transport facilities, lack of information and unclear export regulations. Finally, at the level of the enterprise there is often a lack of technological knowledge, management skills and information about accounting practices.

There are various externally-funded projects that have been able to reduce these obstacles, particularly with regard to credit. Especially interesting is the small revolving loan fund (US\$ 30 000) that UNIFEM allocated to the Mongol Khorshoo (Cooperative) Bank which, in collaboration with the Mongolian Women's Federation, provides small loans to women entrepreneurs. These loans usually are tiny, yet have resulted in an unusually high rate of job-creation, of more than 10 jobs per loan. Employees are mostly family members or former co-workers of the women entrepreneurs and are mostly but not exclusively women. The cost per job created is about US\$ 50.

Since almost all current programmes concentrate on Ulaanbaatar, we recommend that three pilot Local Enterprise Promotion Centres (LEPCs) be set up in *aimag* capital cities. One possibility would be to set up the *aimag* LEPCs as branch offices of existing institutions, such as the Small Enterprise Promotion Centre in Ulaanbaatar. The purpose of the LEPCs is to provide the following services for small enterprises in collaboration with local employment agencies and non-governmental organisations:

- business opportunity studies;
- entrepreneur development training;
- business management training, including the areas of marketing, finance and production;
- training and advice on development of business plans;
- assistance for getting access to credit at local banking institutions or, in the absence of such institutions, provision of credit;
- technical advisory services.[5]

(v) Strengthening Local Employment Agencies

At present, there are 33 self-financing employment agencies at *aimag* (18 agencies), town (3 agencies) and the Ulaanbaatar district level (12 agencies). Because of the heavy workload associated with loan applications and disbursements under the Employment Fund and the processing of job-seekers' registrations and vacancies, personnel resources are clearly insufficient, particularly at the *aimag* level. The staff of employment agencies are not on MPPL's payroll and salaries are paid out of placement fees (which tend to be much smaller at the local level) and perhaps also out of the Employment Fund.

Employment intermediation seems to be most effective in Ulaanbaatar where in 1993 the employment agencies were able to fill 2700 of the 2800 announced vacancies. For the country as a whole in 1993 the employment agencies found jobs for 18 000 out of the 70 000 unemployed. The employment offices have usually little time for vocational counselling or for contacts with employers. They often act as a simple go-between on the basis of the profile of the unemployed person and the vacancy information provided by the employer.

According to estimates of the MPPL, there were about 20 000 unemployed young people in rural areas who have completed 8th and 9th grades. In order to alleviate the problem of rural unemployment, the Ministry started a skill-training programme targeted at unemployed, out-of-school youths. Training was organised through the employment agencies at *aimag* and town levels. A total of 3 million tugriks were spent through the *aimags*, which in turn funded Training and Production Centres (TPCs) to conduct short-cycle (15 days to 6 months) training courses in income-generating skills, such as traditional shoemaking, cooking and food processing. Between 1991 and 1993 more than 6500 youths received training, and there was increasing demand in 1993, despite the fact that trainees had to pay for the training. The experience gained through this programme should be further strengthened by the introduction and adaptation of community-based training methodologies that have been successfully applied in other developing countries.

The registration of job-seekers and vacancies is still carried out by hand (clerically) and this prevents the construction of a national jobs registry and leads to an artificial separation of labour markets, largely along *aimag* lines. There is thus a case for computerising vacancies and registrations of job-seekers; in addition, the restrictions on geographical mobility should be lifted.

Having said this, it must be accepted that employment exchanges and improved labour market information in general are unlikely by themselves to contribute very much to the reduction of the high level of unemployment in Mongolia. The incentive of an unemployed person to register at an employment exchange is weak. It sometimes is not easy to get to an exchange to register and, having registered, the benefits of doing so are few. The exchanges, as we have seen, are unable at present to provide effective assistance to the unemployed in finding a new job nor are they able to mitigate hardship by providing unemployment compensation. In principle, the employer of a laid-off worker is required to provide the nearest labour exchange with a sum equivalent to three months' salary at the full rate. The employment exchange should then pay the laid-off worker four monthly instalments at a rate equal to the minimum living standard (i.e. poverty-line) in effect at the time. These four instalments would of course vary depending on whether the worker lives in a rural or urban area. In practice, however, there are very few beneficiaries. In 1991, only 2.3 per cent of the unemployed received compensation; in 1992, only 1.3 per cent and in 1993 only 0.4 per cent received compensation.[6]

If very few people benefit from registering, it is very likely that not all the unemployed do in fact bother to register; indeed, it is plausible that the figures on registered unemployment measure only the tip of the iceberg. Unemployed first-time job seekers, in particular, are unlikely to register since even in principle they are not entitled to compensation payments. Of course some people who have a job (say, as an illegal trader) may register as being unemployed in the hope that something better may turn up at the labour exchange, but it would seem to be unlikely that the number could be large. On balance our view is that the data on unemployment are in general unreliable and that the official figures probably understate the severity of the problem.

THE SOCIAL SAFETY-NET

A social safety-net is needed for all those who either are not able to work or are not able to find work. Children, pensioners and disabled persons belong to the first category, as well as single mothers without access to child-care facilities who are looking after young children. People who are looking for a job or who are unproductively employed belong to the second category. They may be young unemployed in the *aimags* and towns as well as the many underemployed persons in the rural and urban areas.

Many unemployed and underemployed people could in principle be provided jobs on community-based labour-intensive schemes, some of which could be financed by the Growth, Employment and Poverty Alleviation Fund proposed in Chapter 2. There is also a need for a more labour-intensive approach specifically in construction and physical infrastructure development. Such a combined approach would enable two birds to be killed with one stone: it would provide much-needed employment for the un- and underemployed and it would contribute to the development of a road network and other infrastructure that is desperately needed.

(i) Labour-Intensive Infrastructure and Community-Based Projects

Even if all the measures recommended so far in this chapter are carried out, the employment situation will remain so serious that a major reform in the form of a guaranteed employment scheme should be considered.[7] Many governments have extensive experience in organising public-works projects as a way to reduce seasonal or year-round unemployment while creating useful productive assets. In the state of Maharashtra, India, for example, a successful employment guarantee scheme has been in operation in the rural areas since 1975.

The basic outline of a guaranteed employment scheme is very simple. Any able-bodied person seeking employment and willing to do manual work is guaranteed a job at a subsistence wage. The daily wage-rate or piece-rate is set at a level which does not attract workers from other jobs, since the purpose of the scheme is to provide work to those who have no other source of gainful employment. In the rural areas this means that the wage-rate should be set marginally below, say 10 per cent below, the wages received by hired workers in the lowest-income regions of the province.

We do not recommend that a guaranteed employment scheme be introduced immediately in Mongolia, because sufficient resources at present are not available, but the broad principles of a guaranteed employment scheme could be used when developing the guidelines for labour-intensive infrastructure and community-based projects. There are many activities that could fall under such a programme. In the rural areas there is a great need for bridges, gravel roads, storage facilities, and possibly 'shelter belts'. In the *sums* and *bags* there may be a need for basic facilities such as sanitation. In the cities and towns there may be needs for access streets, street-maintenance, water, street-lighting, garbage-collection, etc.[8] There are many things to be done and many unemployed people willing to do them for a subsistence wage.

The great advantage of community- or area-based projects – many of which could be financed by the Growth, Employment and Poverty Alleviation Fund – is that they can reflect people's needs as articulated by local-level institutions. However, not all local projects are highly labour-intensive (e.g. the installation of diesel generators) but a special effort should be made to employ as many people as possible in the creation of community assets.[9] Of course, when local communities undertake larger programmes such as the construction of bridges and roads, they will need technical advice from *aimag* centres or even from Ulaanbaatar, and provision for this should be included in the scheme.

There is therefore a strong case in favour of a national programme to promote labour and local resource-based approaches in specialised infrastructure projects. Although 'public works' are often part of 'public' investment, an important aspect of an employment-creating strategy is the involvement of the private sector – national consultants, local contractors, target-group institutions and user organisations – in infrastructure and works construction and follow-up activities, particularly maintenance. Such an approach reinforces the development of human capital and national institutional capacity through planning and implementation of projects and programmes at the national and local levels. The Ministry of Roads, Transport and Communications, for example, could promote the labour-intensive construction and maintenance of gravel roads which are needed to connect *aimag* centres.[10]

(ii) The Social Assistance Fund

The government allocated about 5 million tugriks to this fund in 1993, but because of rapidly rising poverty the government plans to allocate 150 million tugriks to the Fund in 1994. The budget allocation for the Assistance Fund is in principle determined according to estimates, surveys and proposals from the *aimags* and the independent towns. The local 'Assistance Council' is responsible for the surveys and for resolving issues regarding the granting of assistance and price discounts for low-income and poor households and citizens. They are helped by the governors of *bags, sums* and *horoos* who are responsible for making detailed surveys, registering poor and very poor households and citizens, monitoring changes in incomes and keeping the social-security divisions informed on a quarterly basis. Each local council consists of 6–7 persons from the social-security departments of *aimags*, capitals and district administrations, and from women's, children's and elderly people's organisations. The councils confer with the governor of their respective administrative level, but the final decision on the allocation of grants is taken by the chairperson of the local social security division.

In March 1994, low-income and poor households were in principle eligible for social assistance when their per capita income (including income in kind) was below Tg. 3200 per month in the urban and Tg. 2900 in the rural areas. (See Chapter 2.) But, in practice, assistance is mostly provided on criteria additional to income. In some northern provinces, for example, assistance was provided to families whose children could not go to school because there was only one pair of winter boots available. Assistance is generally provided to all the disabled and to elderly people without family support, as well as to families under the poverty-line.

The Social Assistance Fund is not dependent exclusively on state allocations; it also accepts donations from firms and private citizens as well as from foreign organisations. Apparently very little cash is given to the recipients of social assistance, except when people are considered 'very poor', i.e. having an income per capita below 40 per cent of the poverty-line. Otherwise, people usually receive – according to circumstances – free lunches, discounts on milk purchased for children, as well as discounts on rent and fuel costs, winter and summer clothes for children, etc. A small part of the Fund is devoted to the provision of short-term loans for buying simple tools and raw materials for running a small business and for engaging in small livestock production and vegetable gardening. Finally, the Fund also subsidises local social welfare institutions such as aid centres, kindergartens and orphanages.

SUMMARY AND CONCLUSIONS

Mongolia's employment situation has deteriorated rapidly since 1989. Registered unemployment has risen to 5 per cent in Ulaanbaatar and to 15–20 per cent in the *aimag* and *sum* centres. Wages have lost more than 50 per cent of their purchasing power, and the incomes of herders have been affected by low livestock prices. As a result of privatisation, employment in the state enterprises has dropped steeply, while employment in informal-sector activities has expanded. Women have generally suffered more from declining employment opportunities than men have.

To improve the incomes of the rural poor three broad steps can be recommended (which are fully developed in Chapters 7 and 8): first, develop conditions for the growth of the livestock sector through market development, infrastructure, and delivery of health and other services; second, develop policies which target the poorest households specifically, through credit schemes, welfare schemes to guarantee fodder, medicines, livestock or draught animals; and third, promote rural small industries based on the processing of agricultural products and the development of rural non-farm activities in general.

The emphasis in urban areas should shift away from large companies and be placed instead on the development of small and medium enterprises in activities that meet the demands of the domestic market. Some of these enterprises ultimately could enter the export market after they have achieved success supplying local consumers and other businesses. The service sector is already showing signs of generating employment in areas such as tourism, business and professional services, and distribution. But small and medium enterprise development is held back by a number of obstacles arising from the general economic environment (inflation and lack of infrastructure for example); from difficulties in obtaining credit; from the limited size of the domestic market and the inaccessibility of export markets; and from the lack of technological knowledge, management skills and accounting practices. We recommend that Local Enterprise Promotion Centres (LEPCs) be created at the *aimag* level in order to overcome some of these obstacles. We also recommend some strengthening of local employment agencies that have to cope with a rising flow of unemployed job-seekers. Information on vacancies and the unemployed should become available outside the *aimag* level. And employment agencies should intensify their placement services and mobilise the unemployed for community-based projects and labour-intensive public works. We recommend that the social safety net be enlarged and strengthened. The best safety net would be a guaranteed employment scheme that would offer employment at a low wage and would be designed in such a way that the beneficiaries would essentially select themselves. In other words, because of the low wage offered, only people who have no other way to obtain employment would be attracted. Within the context of decentralisation to the *aimag* level, we propose the development of community-based projects, many of which could be financed out of the Growth, Employment and Poverty Alleviation Fund recommended in Chapter 2. We also recommend the development of a national scheme that would design and carry out labour-intensive public works. A very good candidate for such a scheme would be the construction of roads, not only between *aimag* cities, but also between *aimag* centres, towns and rural household groups.

A second element of the social safety-net is the continuation and enlargement of the Social Assistance Fund, which is unique to Mongolia and has served a useful purpose. The transition towards a market economy has created poverty among elderly persons, female-headed households, children and the unemployed and they have a right to social support. An enlarged Social Assistance Fund can ensure that they receive that support.

NOTES

1. A mini-survey undertaken in April 1994 shows that 10 out of 20 interviewed small business people in Ulaanbaatar managed to obtain a greater income in the informal sector than in their previous formal-sector job.
2. J. Edstrom (with research assistance from L. Ganzorigt and S. Badarch), 'The Reform of Livestock Marketing in Post-communist Mongolia: Problems for a Food Secure and Equitable Market Development', in *Nomadic Peoples*, 1994.
3. ILO, *Mongolia: Policies for Equitable Transition*, November 1992.
4. J. Magill, C. Lipson and M. McKone, *Mongolia: Options and Strategies for Small- and Medium-Scale Enterprise Development*, Bethesda, GEMINI technical report No. 63, November 1993.

5. For details of the proposal see ILO, *Mongolia: Employment Programme Formulation Report*, Ulaanbaatar, 14–22 March 1994.

6. International Labour Office, *Mongolia: Employment Programme Formulation Report*, Ulaanbaatar, 14–22 March 1994, pp. 11–12.

7. K. Griffin and T. McKinley: *Implementing a Human Development Strategy* (London: Macmillan, 1994), Ch. 5.

8. See: ILO, *From Want to Work. Job creation for the urban poor* (Geneva, 1993).

9. For a more detailed examination, see F. Stewart and W. van der Geest: *Adjustment and Social Funds: Political Panacea or Effective Poverty Reduction?*, Oxford, International Development Centre, Queen Elizabeth House, January 1994; mimeographed.

10. Asian Development Bank, *Mongolia: Economic Reforms and Development Issues*, Ulaanbaatar, Harvard Institute for International Development, 30 April 1993, draft.

4 Human Capital Formation under Conditions of Acute Resource Scarcity

Sheila Smith

Mongolia has an impressively well-developed human resource base, due to the priority given during the socialist period to health and education. In 1989, 96 per cent of the working population (aged 15 and above) were literate, and 7.5 per cent had higher education. The policy of promoting female education was manifested in many ways, with overall achievements in gender equality in education comparing favourably with many middle- and higher-income countries.

In the health sector, high levels of investment resulted in a medical infrastructure which provided effective access to health services by the population despite the low levels of population density. With the expansion of medical coverage, the death rate declined from 12.2 per 1000 to 7.9 during the period 1970–90. However, the pro-natalist policy of the socialist period was associated with a high crude birth rate and relatively high maternal mortality rates.

During the period of transition since 1990, the austerity measures undertaken by the government have involved significant cuts in real levels of expenditure on education and health, with expenditure on education falling by 69 per cent in real terms over the period 1990–92. Expenditures on health also experienced a sharp real decline during 1991–93. These cuts in human capital formation were greater than the fall in total output and income. Thus the share of total resources allocated to health and education declined sharply, in an effort to maintain current consumption.

In the present economic circumstances Mongolia's capacity to deliver basic health and education services is in a state of extreme crisis, and the very significant achievements made by Mongolia in the development of human resources are under serious threat. It is of utmost importance that priority be given to protecting these achievements. There are two major reasons for this. Firstly, Mongolia's human resources are central to the transformation of the Mongolian economy into a dynamic, market-based economic system. Secondly, equitable access to basic health and education services constitutes a major component of well-being for the population as a whole, and in Mongolia such provision has been one of the main reasons for the low levels of poverty during the socialist period. The safeguarding of health and education is therefore of central importance both to economic recovery and to poverty-alleviation.

The strategy proposed involves re-emphasising the importance of investment in human capital, including the importance of gender equality, re-focusing on primary education and primary health care, and strengthening the linkages between human capital formation and the evolving labour market.

This chapter provides an analysis of the education sector, involving an account of Mongolia's past achievements, recent trends occurring during the transition, and the problems which are emerging. Government policies and their implementation are discussed, and finally some conclusions are derived concerning the elements of a strategy to protect access to basic education. Chapter 5 focuses on health, nutrition and population achievements, trends, issues and policies.

EDUCATIONAL ACHIEVEMENTS AND RECENT TRENDS

Mongolia's past achievements in developing her human resource base are outstanding on the basis of international comparisons. The decision to invest a major share of resources in education was wise, since investment in human resources, especially in basic education, yields a higher return than most other investments.[1] In particular, investments which are spread over a larger group of people yield a higher rate of return than investments concentrated more narrowly. Widespread investments also have more equitable and democratic outcomes, particularly because they involve a more equal share of benefits accruing to women.[2]

Mongolia's experience is especially impressive in terms of the very high rates of enrolment and educational achievements among the nomadic population, which is a very significant minority of the people of Mongolia. This has been achieved largely by means of an effective system of boarding schools throughout the country, which have ensured that levels of literacy, numeracy and problem-solving skills among the livestock-herders are as high as among the rest of the population.

Analyses of international experience show clearly that the social rates of return on human development expenditures are very high, and that the social benefits of investment are usually higher at the base of an expenditure pyramid (e.g. primary education) than at the peak (e.g. postgraduate education). Therefore, expenditure on basic education and health can be a very efficient way to promote development. Furthermore, a healthy, literate and skilled labour force is the foundation of a country's long-term growth. But the benefits of investing in people go beyond the increase in labour productivity: a healthy and well-educated citizenry contributes to the social cohesion of a country and to the dynamism of all aspects of life and culture.[3]

The socialist period in Mongolia was characterised by extremely high gross enrolment rates: in 1989 these were 98 per cent in primary schools, 85 per cent in secondary schools and 15 per cent in tertiary education. In addition, enrolment of girls is high: in 1993, girls accounted for 54 per cent of enrolments in primary and secondary schools, and 64 per cent in higher education institutions. The total enrolment in 1992 at all levels of education was nearly half a million, or one-quarter of the total population.

These high levels of educational attainment had been achieved by heavy investment in education: in 1990, education accounted for 25 per cent of government expenditures and 16 per cent of GDP. After the termination of Soviet assistance and the collapse of the CMEA, overall public expenditure was cut from 64 per cent of GDP in 1990 to 58 per cent in 1991 and 33 per cent in 1992. The percentage decrease in expenditure on education was larger than the decline in either GDP or total public expenditure. Between 1990 and 1992, total public spending fell by 58 per cent in real terms, while the allocation to education was cut by 69 per cent during the same period. The austerity measures in education have included halting capital investment and introducing partial cost-recovery in kindergarten and rural boarding schools.

The Ministry of Science and Education, in its Education and Human Resource Masterplan, states that the basic education system is in a state of crisis, with enrolments declining dramatically, drop-out rates rising, teachers leaving, and schools deteriorating, and that the educational crisis is most serious in rural areas.[4]

The most pressing problem of current concern is the drop-out rate in primary and secondary schools, which rose from 0.8 per cent in 1989 to 4.9 per cent in 1991–2. A World Bank mission estimated that in 1993 approximately 105 000 or 23 per cent of children who should be in grades 1–8 were not in school.[5] Enrolments show a downward trend from 1990 onwards at all levels of education. The gross enrolment rate in Grades 1–3 fell from 100 per cent in 1989 to 74–83 per cent by the end of 1992.[6] There is a linkage between rising drop-out rates and the higher opportunity cost of children in rural areas which has resulted from increased use of children's labour following the privatisation of the herds. School attendance has also suffered from the effects of the rising contribution levied on parents to cover costs of food and clothing. There is also a linkage of drop-out rates to urban unemployment and poverty in the cities. Overall, rural areas have been affected more severely than urban areas by the drop-out problem,[7] and more remote *aimags* have been affected more than the *aimags* closer to the major cities and railway line, with boarding schools affected more severely than other schools. Enrolment of boarders in 1992 was half the 1989 level. According to a DANIDA study of the dropout problem, there is a significant overrepresentation of boys. A further dimension of the problem is that it is more serious among younger children aged 8–11 than among older children.[8]

The rising drop-out rate and falling enrolments will result in rising rates of illiteracy and semi-literacy, and will lead to the current generation being less well-educated than their parents.[9]

CURRENT GOVERNMENT GOALS AND POLICIES

The protection of universal access to basic education is the priority of the Government of Mongolia. The Education Law of 1991 envisages compulsory basic education (defined as eight years of schooling, consisting of six years of primary and two years of middle-school education). The constitution of Mongolia, approved in 1992, guarantees the right to education, and stipulates that 'the State shall provide basic general education free'.[10]

The Ministry of Science and Education, with the support of the Asian Development Bank, conducted an Education and Human Resources Master Planning exercise between October and December 1993. The resulting Master Plan was adopted as official government policy and was signed by the Minister in March 1994. There is a draft Education Law currently under discussion, which includes many of the proposals in the Master Plan.

According to the Master Plan, Mongolia wishes to preserve and enhance the equity and effectiveness of the results of basic and general secondary education. Basic education would continue to involve eight years of education, but these would consist of the last two years of kindergarten plus grades 1–6 of formal education. We understand, however, that the government has decided not to accept this feature of the Master Plan and hence not to amend the 1991 Education Law. Thus the eight compulsory years of schooling will remain as six years of primary and two years of middle school; no years of kindergarten will be compulsory. Primary and middle-school levels of education would be the responsibility of government. Parents and communities would be encouraged to assist schools in terms of financial help, labour, materials or supplies.

Further goals include the provision of social assistance to children without parents and to children from economically disadvantaged families to permit them to benefit from education.

Achievement of the goals of protecting universal access to basic education requires strategies towards finance and priorities, as well as a restructuring of the form and content of education to use shrinking resources more effectively and to enhance the relevance of education, especially to rural livelihoods. Protecting access to basic education also requires a strategy towards children of poor women, whose access is fragile in present conditions, and towards vulnerable groups, particularly children in especially difficult circumstances.

In the sphere of finance, continued overall budgetary stringency is likely for some years. However, three issues should be addressed with some urgency: first, the relationship between the national education budget and the expenditure on education at *aimag* and *sum* levels; secondly, the urgency of maintaining the financial viability of boarding schools during the period of development of alternative forms of provision; and thirdly, the priorities and allocation of resources within the education budget.

Concerning the relationship between national and local education budgets, although basic education is financed from the national budget, there is not a clear relationship between sectoral allocation in the national budget and sectoral allocation at *aimag* and *sum* levels. This is because the *aimags* and *sums* have some autonomy in the allocation of resources received from the national budget. According to the Education and Human Resource Master Plan, schools in some *sums* are receiving less than they should, because the *aimag* and *sum* levels may cut the allocation for education below what is allocated by the State Khural.[11] Thus, in order to maintain minimum national standards in primary education, the rights and responsibilities of local government in the allocation of funds needs to be more carefully defined. This is of particular importance for poverty-alleviation, since budgetary stringency is likely to be most acute in the poorest areas, which will have least capacity to supplement budgetary allocations with contributions from parents and the community.

The second financial issue which needs to be addressed is the viability of boarding schools, which have been extremely important in educational provision for children of nomadic households in the past. Enrolments in boarding schools have fallen, in part because of the dramatic increases in heating and food costs, which in turn have been passed on as charges to parents, and in part because of increases in demand for child (especially boys') labour. It is essential that means be sought to maintain the viability of such schools, even if this is a temporary strategy. This is because Mongolia's success in delivering education to her nomadic population has been achieved thanks to the effectiveness of the boarding-school system, and until alternative means of educational provision have been developed, the boarding schools should not be allowed to collapse. This is a top priority.

For the future, there are questions concerning the cost-effectiveness of boarding schools, particularly in view of the budgetary stringency which will continue to constrain educational provision, and serious examination of this question is needed. This issue will be discussed further below, in the context of the structure and content of education.

The third financial issue is that of priorities within the education budget. In conditions of budgetary stringency, which are likely to remain severe for some time, the issue of priorities within the education budget becomes an issue of major significance. The key priority in these circumstances is basic and general education to enable all children to acquire literacy, numeracy and problem-solving skills, both to enhance their ability to participate in the economy and society, and as a basis for continuing education in the future. There is room for reallocation within the education budget from tertiary and vocational to primary education.[12] As indicated in Table 4.1, data for 1992 indicate that, although 84.4 per cent of all students are enrolled in primary and general secondary schools, only 55 per cent of educational expenditure is allocated to these levels of education. In contrast, kindergartens (ages 3–7) account for 12.9 per cent of students and 21 per cent of expenditure, higher education for 0.4 per cent of students and 16 per cent of expenditure, and vocational secondary education for 2.3 per cent of students and 7 per cent of expenditure.[13] For every student in higher education, expenditure is 6.37 times expenditure per

TABLE 4.1 The distribution of educational expenditure, 1992

	Government expenditure (%)	Students (%)	Government expenditure per student (tugriks)	Index of expenditure per student (tugriks)
1. Kindergarten	21	12.9	5 094	250
2. Basic and general secondary education	55	84.4	2 035	100
3. Vocational secondary education	7	2.3	9 333	459
4. Higher education	16	0.4	12 954	637

Source: Based on data in Government of Mongolia, *Mongolia Education and Human Resources Master Plans*, 6 December 1993.

student in primary and general secondary schools; for every child in kindergarten, expenditure is 2.5 times expenditure per student in primary and general secondary education.

The allocation of resources within the educational pyramid is an issue of crucial significance. Not only are the costs per pupil in primary and general secondary education lower than in tertiary education, but the relative benefits are higher, and hence the return on investment in education rises as one moves from the top to the bottom of the pyramid. The diversion of even modest sums from universities can have magnified effects on primary education.[14]

Thus, in order to protect the access and quality of basic education in Mongolia, there is a strong case for reallocation, as other means may be sought for financing vocational and higher education, involving parental contributions, the private sector and external donor support. In the case of kindergartens, it is imperative that more cost-effective means of maintaining access be sought. During the transition period, parents have been required to contribute 50 per cent of the costs of kindergartens, and this has resulted in a sharp fall in enrolments. This has serious consequences of three kinds: first, many children are receiving no education during their most receptive years; secondly, the health and nutrition status of children was positively affected by kindergarten attendance and this is now being threatened by falling enrolments; and thirdly, women's labour-force participation is being undermined. There is a strong case for including at least some years of kindergarten education within the definition of basic education to be provided free to all children.

Closely related to the allocation of resources among levels of education is the issue of the form and content of education, which needs to be restructured in order to promote more effective use of limited resources, as well as to enhance the perceived relevance of education and therefore reverse the problem of drop-outs from the demand side. As discussed above, one reason for the falling enrolments and rising drop-out rates is the increased cost of sending children to school. This is partly an increase in direct costs (charges for food, fuel and clothing), partly an increase in opportunity cost (because privatisation of herds has led to rising demand for child labour). But a further important factor seems to be the lack of conviction by parents about the benefits of education. This may be linked to the reduction in demand for skilled labour during the transition period, and certainly the demand for schooling is closely related to labour market conditions and overall economic growth.

However, the issue of the relevance of education in current circumstances seems to be more fundamental than this. It concerns the perception, particularly by herders, that education is not necessary for the life their children will lead. In terms of private calculations of costs and benefits this may be a rational decision. However, the social benefits of education are greater than the private benefits, and in the case of livestock, for example, which is one of the key sectors in the economic recovery of Mongolia, basic education is vital to the growth of productivity and incomes, given the need for new skills in understanding, calculating, negotiating and coping in a market economy. This is additional to the benefits in terms of greater mobility, wider choices and receptivity to further training which basic education confers. The issue of education for a market economy also needs to be addressed in school curricula generally.

Given the choices currently being made by many parents, especially in rural areas, to withdraw their children from school or not to enrol them at all, there is a need to adapt the content of education more to local conditions. This could partly be done by involving communities more in decisions about the types of educational provision which are most appropriate. The role of the Ministry of Science and Education would be to identify a range of options, such as distance education, peripatetic teachers who would serve a number of settlements, *bag* schools, etc., and to develop the methodologies, materials and training programmes. It may also be necessary to reform the content of education, increasing the science content to include health, biology, veterinarian knowledge, earth science and environmental science, even though considerable progress has already been made in these areas. Protecting access to basic education by poor women and to children in female-headed households is an issue of particular concern during the transition. Approximately 72 per cent of single heads of households, mostly female-headed, are below the poverty-line and are generally poorly skilled. Around 20 000–40 000 households are headed by women.[15] There is a need for better gender-disaggregated data on the relationships between poverty, education, skills and employment, and for skills-training to be targeted at poor women. As discussed above, the transition has also dramatically increased costs of child care, which is costly to the economy, as women's labour-force participation (and their ability to participate in training programmes) is linked to accessibility and affordability of child care. The collapse of affordable child care and daycare is associated with higher unemployment rates among women than among men, as women can no longer afford the costs of kindergartens: 54 per cent of the registered unemployed are women.[16]

More generally, the access of children from poor households requires a better-funded social assistance system which provides clothing and school materials systematically to such children. A well-functioning system of identification of poor households and of their needs is in place, but the availability of resources is extremely limited.

The access by the poor to basic education also requires a strategy towards children in especially difficult circumstances. During the transition there appear to be increasing problems of child neglect, abandonment and destitution. A 1992 survey indicated that there were more than 10 000 orphans and 39 000 single-parent children who were separated from their families. In 1992, there were about 600 registered street-children, and their numbers seem to be increasing.[17] There are also problems of children with disabilities, of which there are an estimated 40 000.[18] Provision for disabled children is very limited. DANIDA estimates that only between 10 and 15 per cent of disabled children receive any education at all. The special education available is generally in segregated schools or classes. Coverage could be greatly expanded by integrating special education into the ordinary school system. There is a DANIDA project to assist with new curricula and new methodologies to enable integration and thereby expanded provision, aiming at 80 per cent coverage.[19] The National Programme of Action for the Development of Children in the 1990s, approved by the government in May 1993, envisages several measures for improving care, protection and rehabilitation of children in especially difficult circumstances. These include increasing the number of orphanages, strengthening non-institutional approaches such as foster care, enhancing facilities for vocational training, and facilitating participation of poor children in education by providing free clothing, textbooks and other school materials.[20]

IMPLEMENTING GOVERNMENT POLICIES

Institutional arrangements within the education sector are still changing, and may change further with the new Education Law. However, certain changes have taken place which are unlikely to be reversed, in particular the decentralisation process. The authority of the Ministry of Science and Education (MOSE) to direct educational development was reduced by the Educational Law of 1991, which gives greater responsibility to authorities at city, *aimag*, *sum*, district and lower levels.[21] MOSE has lost many of its former operational duties, and is now responsible for basic planning and policy formulation, including master planning and policy analysis at national level, and provision of planning-support services; programme approval and institutional development; system-wide personnel development; evaluation and assessment services. These require new capacities.

There seems to have been little involvement of communities in the discussion of educational reforms, but it is clear that more community involvement is needed to adapt school organisation more to local needs and circumstances. Community involvement will also be vital in overcoming the problem of falling school enrolments as well as reforming education to use resources more effectively.

Policy capacity at national level needs to be increased to develop policies, and to implement and monitor policies. At present the MOSE has only 61 staff at its headquarters, roughly only half of which is devoted to education issues and the other half to science. This clearly is not sufficient to develop and implement a major reform programme with new educational structures, new approaches to education (such as distance teaching), new curricula and textbooks. Capacities to be developed would include policy-analysis skills, including an improved information system and the capacity to utilize it effectively. Capacities at city, *aimag* and *sum* level may also need to be enhanced in financial, technical and management skills, given the greater decentralisation of responsibility.

SUMMARY AND CONCLUSIONS

Mongolia's education system is in a state of deep crisis, and concerted efforts are needed to protect access by Mongolian children to basic education. Not only is the economic case for investment in human capital an overwhelming one, but the contribution of access to basic education to the alleviation of poverty cannot be overestimated. There is thus a strong case for a reallocation of national resources in favour of the education sector as a whole. This should be a matter of very high priority.

During the transition there is evidence that Mongolia's past impressive achievements in human resource development are under serious threat. Enrolments have been declining, drop-out rates rising, teachers leaving and schools deteriorating. The crisis is most serious in rural areas. These trends must be reversed with some urgency.

Mongolia's Master Plan for Education and Human Resources contains many proposals to address these urgent issues. The following are of paramount importance:

(i) In the sphere of finance, there is a need for clarification of the rights and responsibilities of MOSE, *aimags* and *sums* concerning budgetary allocations to education, to strengthen the relationship between sectoral allocation at national level and sectoral allocation at *aimag* and *sum* levels, and to safeguard equity and minimum national standards of educational provision. This is proposed in the Education and Human Resource Master Plan 1993, and is a vital component of a policy to protect equity and minimum education provision throughout the country.

(ii) Within the education sector, highest priority should be given to basic education, including primary education plus two years of middle-school education. This is also proposed in the Education and Human Resource Master Plan. This will involve a significant reallocation of resources from vocational and higher education towards primary and middle-school education, while seeking alternative forms of funding of vocational and tertiary education.

(iii) The relevance of educational content to the emerging economic structure needs to be enhanced, with an emphasis on the skills needed in a market economy. An intense effort is needed to further develop strategies for educational reform. These would involve the Ministry of Science and Education in identifying and developing a range of options for educational provision, such as distance teaching, peripatetic teachers, multi-subject and multi-grade teachers, *bag* schools and *ger* schools from which localities can choose. The Master Plan proposes to develop such options, but it is essential that resources are mobilised not only to develop such options but to make them available nationally, with funds for distributing materials, retraining teachers, etc. DANIDA has provided support for such activities, but the level of investment in educational reform needs to be increased. Furthermore, although expenditure of resources on education in Mongolia is an extremely effective use of overseas aid, DANIDA has announced that it will discontinue assistance to Mongolia after 1996. Thus alternative means of financing these activities needs to be sought with some urgency.

(iv) It is essential that decision-making on educational options is decentralised. This should be done by involvement of communities in discussions and decisions, so that the form of educational provision is adapted to local conditions.

(v) In the immediate future, resources should be sought to enable boarding schools to continue to function, since these have been and still are the means of delivering education to the children of nomadic people. The current system must be kept functioning while alternatives are being developed. Within basic education, this is the highest priority. Since boarding schools have been extraordinarily successful in the past, perhaps an in-depth evaluation would be warranted, which would indicate in detail the costs and cost-effectiveness of such schools. This could serve as the basis for comparison with alternatives, and hence would enable better-informed decisions. The possibility of continued reliance on boarding schools in certain localities should remain open. It may be possible to explore the optimum seasonality of schooling, to coincide with periods of less intense demand for labour. Although this would imply schooling during the winter when heating costs are higher, the subsidisation of heating costs may be the lowest cost means of ensuring continued high levels of enrolment and attendance among the nomadic population.

(vi) To protect the access of poor women and of their children to education, affordable and accessible child-care facilities, including kindergartens, need to be provided when resources permit, possibly by means of lower-cost approaches such as child-minders. This is of particular importance in urban areas. Better gender-disaggregated data are needed to enable targeting of training towards poor women.

(vii) In order to ensure access to education by poor children, resources need to be mobilised to enable the present social assistance system to provide poor households with support in the form of clothing and school materials. This will be included in the proposed Growth, Employment and Poverty Alleviation Fund, discussed in Chapter 2.

(viii) Concerning institutional arrangements, there is a need for greater involvement of communities in discussions and decisions about the form of educational provision and its content. Policy and management capacity at national, *aimag* and *sum* levels needs to be strengthened.

(ix) The role of donors would be twofold: technical and capital assistance. The priorities for donor support in the form of technical assistance should be to support MOSE's planning and management capacity, to enhance management capacity at *aimag* and *sum* levels, to support the development and dissemination of a range of cost-effective options for educational forms and structures, to support the reform of curricula, and to assist in the establishment of a market-oriented approach to vocational and technical education. Technical assistance resources could also be sought for an in-depth evaluation of the boarding schools, of their costs and cost-effectiveness, on the basis of which choices among alternative means of educational delivery can be made. Technical assistance could also be provided for a feasibility study for low-cost options for insulating school buildings and adapting them for the use of traditional methods of heating.

In the short-to-medium term, support should be provided to enable boarding schools to continue to function, by supplying fuel, food (for example from the World Food Programme, the UN programme which provides food aid) and transport costs. This would be temporary, during which time alternative and more cost-effective methods and structures are being developed.

Capital assistance should be provided for improving supplies of essential imported inputs such as paper, printing and duplicating equipment.

NOTES

1. See, for example, George Psacharopoulos, 'Returns to Investment in Education', World Bank, Policy Research Working Paper No. 1067, January 1993.
2. See Keith Griffin and Terry McKinley, *Implementing a Human Development Strategy* (London: Macmillan, 1994), Ch. 3.
3. Ibid., p. 35.
4. Ministry of Science and Education, *Mongolia Education and Human Resource Master Plan (1994–1998)*, December 1993, pp. 14ff.
5. Now that parents have to bear more of the costs of educating their children, a generational conflict has emerged: the benefits of education accrue to the children in the future; but many of the costs (opportunity cost of child labour, user charges and food for children in boarding schools) are borne by the parents.
6. World Bank, *Mongolia: Financing Education During Economic Transition*, by Kim Bing Wu, Washington, October 1993.
7. See D. Munhoo, *Current Situation of Mongolian Women and Their Goals in Near Future*, Paper prepared for the National Seminar on Women's Issues, p. 7.
8. See UNICEF, *The Situation of Children and Women in Mongolia*, Ulaanbaatar, December 1993, p. 26, and DANIDA, *School Dropout in Mongolia*, by D. Khokh, M. Ganbat, L. Urantsetseg, S. Dunchee, N. Egelund, P. Schultz-Joergensen and H. Soeberg, undated.
9. Ministry of Science and Education, op. cit., p. 17.
10. UNICEF, op. cit., p. 28.
11. Ministry of Science and Education, op. cit., p. 58.
12. See Ministry of Science and Education, op. cit., and World Bank, 1993, op. cit., p. 22.
13. Calculated from data in Ministry of Science and Education, op. cit.
14. See Griffin and McKinley, op. cit., pp. 44ff.
15. See Barbara Skapa, *Sector Study: Mongolia Women in Development*, Briefing Paper, Asian Development Bank, October 1993.
16. Ibid.
17. UNICEF, op. cit., p. 29.
18. Ibid.
19. DANIDA, *Support to the National Special Education Programmes in Mongolia*, Proposal, August 1993.
20. UNICEF, op. cit., p. 29.
21. Ministry of Science and Education, op. cit., p. 10.

5 Human Capital: The Health and Well-Being of the Population

Sheila Smith and Joyce Lannert

Mongolia's past emphasis on human capital formation was reflected in the priority given to investment in the health of her people. The health sector accounted for between 7.5 and 8.5 per cent of total government expenditure during the period 1980 to 1990, and for 6.7 per cent of GDP in 1990. During the socialist period, major advances in health care were achieved, particularly in the extension of effective health services to the nomadic population.

Because of the high levels of investment in health and the development of an infrastructure to provide health services throughout the sparsely populated countryside, indicators of health among the population show that there was significant progress. Life expectancy rose steadily during the last 40 years, and was estimated in 1985–90 to be 61.3 years.

During the period of transition, falling incomes and cuts in government expenditure have been reflected in expenditure on health, even though the share of total government expenditure allocated to the health sector has not fallen, and in 1991 and 1992 had risen to 12.2 and 14.4 per cent respectively. These increased percentages, however, have been associated with a sharp decline in real levels of expenditure.

As in the education sector, the health care system in Mongolia is confronting a major crisis at present, and past achievements are threatened with reversal. The acute shortage of funds is likely to deepen in the near future. Health facilities have begun to shed staff, patients are expected to provide their own meals and pay for their own drugs, and vehicles are increasingly non-operational due to lack of funds for repairs and petrol, thus making emergency transport impossible and undermining the routine access of the rural population to health-care services.

It has been argued in Chapter 4 that safeguarding the health and education of the population should receive priority in the immediate future. This is partly because Mongolia's human resources are the major basis on which economic recovery and transformation will take place, but it is also because equitable access to basic health and education services has contributed significantly to the low levels of poverty experienced by the Mongolian population in the past. Thus, protecting access to basic health and education services is of central importance both to economic recovery and to poverty alleviation.

This chapter provides an account of achievements in the health sector, in nutrition and in population policy. The chapter contains a review of recent trends occurring during the transition, and of the problems which are emerging. Government policies are discussed, and some conclusions provided concerning a strategy for protecting access to basic health care, safeguarding the nutritional status of the population, and improving the effectiveness of population policy.

THE HEALTH SECTOR: ACHIEVEMENTS AND RECENT TRENDS

Mongolia's achievements in the field of health are as outstanding as those in education, particularly in extending coverage to the scattered, remote nomadic population. As was argued in Chapter 4 in the case of education, investment in health care is a wise use of resources, as rates of return are comparable to or higher than most other investments.

Likewise, there is an inverted pyramid in the case of health as in the case of education. In many countries, a large proportion of the health budget is spent on urban hospitals, while rural people have little access to the formal health-care system.[1] It has been demonstrated clearly that expenditure on preventive care for the population as a whole, for example immunisation programmes, is far more cost-effective than expensive curative care available only to a small minority of the population. Beyond the immediate benefits of expanded public health programmes, there are longer-term benefits, not only for individuals but for society as a whole in the form of fewer days lost from illness, higher labour productivity and increased household incomes. However, unlike most educational deficiencies, which can to some extent be corrected later in life, many health-care problems cannot be corrected in later years, and their negative effects on incomes and well-being can last a lifetime. In some cases the health problems are passed from one generation to the next, e.g. problems of low birth-weight.[2]

Unlike many developing countries, Mongolia's past strategy towards health care followed the reasoning above, with an emphasis on primary health care, involving widespread access to preventive care. The immunisation programme grew steadily during the 1980s, and coverage levels well above 80 per cent were reported from 1989 to 1991.[3] Free ante-natal care and delivery services were also provided, with most births taking place in maternity hospitals.

The system of health-care delivery in rural areas rests to an important extent on *feldshers*, who are paramedical rural health workers with two years of training at one of the three medical colleges in Darkhan city, in Dornogobi *aimag* and in Gobi-Altai *aimag*. About 150 *feldshers* were produced a year. Each *bag*, having between 50 and 100 families, has one *feldsher*, whose responsibility is to make periodic visits to each family in the *bag*, to provide routine preventive care, including immunisation, health education, and simple curative care. *Feldshers* usually have a horse, less often a motorcycle, for transportation.[4]

At the *sum* level, there are hospitals with up to three physicians, two to four *feldshers*, three to four nurses and one pharmacist. They have 10–15 beds. In addition, maternity rest-homes are located near the *sum* hospitals, to which women could go two weeks prior to expected delivery in order to ensure that delivery would take place in a hospital. Inter-*sum* hospitals provide services for 2–3 districts (40–60 beds), with more specialists than are available at *sum* level.

In *aimag* and city centres primary-level care is provided by clinics with an internist, a pediatrician and an obstetrics and gynaecology specialist. Each *aimag* has a general hospital with 250–400 beds which serves both urban and rural populations. (Ulaanbaatar has four general hospitals.) In addition, the *aimag* hospitals provide specialised outpatient clinics (e.g. dental care, treatment of venereal diseases) and emergency services.

During the transition period, serious deterioration has taken place in the health service delivery system. The number of hospital admissions fell from 584 000 in 1988 to 493 000 in 1991, and outpatient consultations fell from 16.4 million in 1988 to 12 million in 1991. Doctor consultations per person fell from 8.0 in 1988 to 4.79 in 1992. These reductions may reflect the shortages of drugs in medical institutions and the decreased sickness allowance given to all employed people from the social insurance fund.[5]

Of the previously-existing 320 maternity hostels, 50 per cent have now closed, since they used to be maintained by the agricultural farms and cooperatives. Responsibility for these hostels has been transferred to the local administrations, whose resources are inadequate. Since the closure of hostels, and due to the decreasing availability of transport to bring women to the hospitals in time for delivery, an increasing number of deliveries are taking place at home. This is one of the explanations given for the rising maternal mortality rate, which rose from 140 per 100 000 in 1985,[6] to 144 and 205 per 100 000 in 1990 and 1992 respectively.[7] The percentage of women who now experience births unattended by any health provider is rising, particularly in rural areas. The increasing incidence of abortions is a further explanation of the rise in the maternal mortality rate, as abortions seem to be used as a form of contraception in the absence of access to other means. It has also been suggested that the quality of care and observation by doctors has been below standard. A further alarming feature of the rising levels of maternal mortality is the disproportionately large numbers of low-literacy mothers (50 per cent) and unemployed mothers (25 per cent).[8] Given the rising levels of unemployment, especially among women, and increasing school drop-out rates, these problems will intensify unless urgent action is taken.

At present, the most pressing problems of current concern in the health sector are morbidity and mortality among mothers and children. The main causes of mortality can be significantly reduced by means of cost-effective primary health-care programmes. Since Mongolia has the health-service infrastructure in place to carry out such programmes, it is feasible to reallocate resources to ensure that primary health care services remain effective, by emphasising preventive care, the availability of necessary equipment and drugs, and ensuring transport facilities. The increases in maternal mortality are a serious warning that the problems arising during the economic transition are fatal and irreversible.

In addition, since the delivery of primary health-care services is dependent on the availability of transport services, the deterioration in access to transport is one of the most serious threats to the health-care system in rural areas. According to Dr B. Orgil, General Director of the Department for Medical Care, Ministry of Health, 27 out of 310 *sum* hospitals have no transportation, and an additional 60–70 have transportation but it is not working.

The urgency of maintaining Mongolia's primary health-care delivery system cannot be overemphasised. Without a healthy population, the prospects for economic recovery will be grim indeed, and as health services deteriorate, the access of the poor will deteriorate most sharply, and as their healthiness diminishes, their ability to engage in income-earning activities or training, or to participate in any aspect of economic, social or political life will also diminish.

CURRENT GOVERNMENT GOALS AND POLICIES

The health policy of the present government, as adopted by the State
Great Khural in 1991, includes the following objectives: to strengthen
preventive and curative health care with emphasis on prevention; to
strengthen health institutions, especially in rural areas; to intensify
maternal and child-health activities with a view to reducing maternal
and infant mortality; to encourage health promotional activities including
family planning; and to provide for a health insurance scheme.[9]

In the review of the health sector conducted in June 1992 by the
Ministry of Health, with the collaboration of the World Health Organisation, the World Bank and the Asian Development Bank, the gross
inadequacy of the facilities available at different levels was revealed,
especially in rural areas. At the first organisational level (*bag*), in order to enable the system to function effectively, the following would
be needed: transport equipment, radio communication equipment and
small-sized examination and diagnostic equipment. At the second organisational level (*sum*), buildings need to be rehabilitated and transport equipment provided, as well as equipment and instruments for
examination, diagnosis and treatment. At the third organisational level
(*aimag* and city), re-equipping is necessary, plus improvement in the
information system to and from *sum* and *aimag*. The government has
prepared a proposal and submitted it to donor representatives and
agencies, envisaging a donor input of $12.6 million. It is expected
that, at the end of the project period, the quality and coverage of rural
health services will have been improved.[10]

Even with the support of external agencies, the effectiveness of the
health-service delivery system is largely dependent on the level and
distribution of national health expenditure. The overall allocation of
central government funding to the health sector has fallen dramatically in real terms, and this is likely to continue. The health sector has
been affected particularly severely by the devaluation of the tugrik
and the withdrawal of assistance from the Soviet Union, since the import
content of health care has been rather high. The budgets for all preventive and curative care at *aimag* and *sum* levels are drawn up at
aimag level, and health care must therefore compete with other pressing local needs. It would therefore seem essential that the allocation
of expenditure within the health-care sector be examined carefully.
Although data are somewhat patchy, Ministry of Health data reported
in the Health Sector Review reveal the following: city and *aimag* hospitals account for 60 per cent on average of current health expenditures

since 1985; inter-*sum* hospitals for 4–6 per cent of the total; *sum* hospitals for 14–17 per cent; *feldshers'* posts for between 1.3 and 1.7 per cent; crèches for 11–12 per cent, and other services for between 6.6 and 7.7 per cent.[11] There would seem to be some room for reallocation downwards, to augment the resources available at *feldsher* level.

In addition, there is room for more cost-effective use of resources. According to the Health Sector Review conducted by the Ministry of Health in 1992, reforms in the health-care system will need to address inefficiencies in resource-use under the health system while protecting and building on the positive aspects of the previous system. A number of areas of cost-saving were identified, including overprescription of drugs, irrational treatment procedures, overspecialisation of services, excessive use of referral services, and over-utilisation of hospitals by patients.

The share of capital expenditure in total health spending seems not to have been severely cut, remaining at around 12 per cent up to 1992.[12] However, it is clear that the level of capital expenditure is not adequate to maintain the functioning of the health-care delivery system, especially in the area of transport equipment.

The mechanisms of financing health care are in the process of reform, and the choice of mechanism will also affect the allocation of resources within the sector, as different mechanisms will be associated with different levels of administrative costs. The recently introduced health insurance scheme, for example, seems to involve at least two negative features: it is administratively costly; and it constitutes a tax on labour, which discourages employment in the private sector and is economically inefficient. In addition, given that the state is paying the insurance costs of a very significant proportion of the population, it does not appear to be an effective means of raising more funds for health care. Since the state is paying all of the costs of groups such as herders, it is also inequitable since not all herders are poor. It would be more efficient and more equitable, as well as less administratively costly, to finance health care from more progressive taxation, combined with certain user charges from which the poorest would be exempt. It obviously is too late to correct the situation now, but it is a pity that the implications of the health-finance system for employment-creation and poverty were not considered before legislation was passed.

NUTRITION

During the post-1945 period, state farming enterprises undoubtedly had a positive effect on nutrition both in terms of food security and increasing the variety of food consumed, primarily increasing the amount of grain in the diet. Before that time there was a small crop-production sector, but with little impact on the majority of pastoral nomads.[13]

Mongolia's move away from a centrally-planned economy, with its state agricultural enterprises and herder collectives (*negdels*) has threatened the food security of three vulnerable groups in particular: pregnant women, especially the rural poor; children; and the elderly poor.

Baseline surveys on the nutritional status of adults do not exist, so it is not possible to compare changes in their nutritional status before and during the transition to a market economy. Birth weights and anthropometric measurements of children under five years old suggest that the macronutrient status of both children and women has been relatively good in the past, but has clearly begun to deteriorate, and in vulnerable families, it has become significantly worse.[14]

The first information about the nutritional status of children was contained in UNICEF's *The Situation of Children and Women in Mongolia* in 1990. A survey of child nutrition was carried out by UNICEF in October 1992, which provided a baseline for comparison in the future. However, there have been no such surveys undertaken for the adult population.

The nutritional status of women has been imputed from other factors related to their child-bearing role: low birth-weight (under 2.5K) of an infant correlates with the mother's poor nutritional status. Due to the high percentage of in-hospital births (98 per cent) through the accessibility to *sum* hospitals, information on birth-weight is available. The incidence of low birth-weight has been increasing during the period 1988 to 1992, from 3.4 per cent of all births to 4.5 per cent in 1990[15] and 6 per cent in 1992.[16] The prevalence of iron-deficiency anaemia in pregnant women is considered to be as high as 40 per cent.[17] However, although the derivative data on maternal nutrition are useful, the limitations of such data are that they are applicable only to pregnant women and do not provide information about the health status of women as a whole, much less about the health status of poor women.

Since information has been collected on the status of child nutrition since 1988 we have a better picture of this status. There are four main nutritional problems for children: protein-energy malnutrition (PEM), vitamin D deficiency, iodine-deficiency disorders and iron-deficiency anaemia. The three measurements of PEM – weight-for-age (W/A), height-for-age (H/A) and weight-for-height (W/H) – measure conditions of underweight, stunting and wasting, respectively.

In Mongolia, the incidence of low W/A occurs most frequently in children aged 13–24 months, which may reflect weaning practices, and more frequently among children in *gers* in *aimags*, especially rural *aimags*, than among those living in flats.[18]

A high prevalence of growth-stunting (H/A) is usually associated with chronically poor socio-economic conditions. The highest incidence of stunting also occurs among the same population of children as W/A – with a disparity of 30 per cent more in *ger* children than flat children.[19]

W/H, or wasting, is an indicator of acute malnutrition. The prevalence of severe malnutrition among Mongolian children is 2.4 per cent, with children between 1 and 2 years of age comprising the most vulnerable group.[20]

Nutrition surveys have demonstrated that there is a high correlation between malnutrition and low educational attainment of the parents, that is, the low human capital of one generation can be passed on to the next. Since the highest incidence of nutritional deficiency occurs in very young children, part of this might be attributable to a lack of education on the part of mothers and health workers about breast-feeding and weaning practices. The optimal approach is to breast-feed exclusively for the first 4–6 months and to continue breast-feeding up to the age of one year.

At present, nutrition education materials observed in hospitals and feeding guidelines and nutrition information on wall posters are not very useful. The contents are too scientific to have meaningful daily application (e.g. vitamin A, carotene). Also the feeding guidelines for each age group are often quite unrealistic (40 grams of apple twice daily, 3–5 drops of lemon juice).

Although statistical data are not available about the specific nutritional status of the elderly poor, there is ample but unsystematic empirical evidence. Nutrition problems among the elderly appear to be pervasive among the herder population after the dissolution of the *negdels* and the disappearance of the social safety-net they provided for the elderly poor. *Aimag* governments operate homes for these people, but the *sums* have waiting lists of others who cannot be accommodated. In Ulaanbaatar there are a few soup kitchens run by private organisations, but how widespread they are in other cities or *aimags* is unknown.

POPULATION POLICY

During the socialist period, in response to perceived under-population, Mongolia had a determinedly pro-natalist population policy. Abortion was illegal, although not uncommon, and contraceptives were mostly unavailable. Mothers were given medals (Order of Mothers' Glory I, II) upon delivery of their fifth and eighth child respectively. Total fertility rates reached 7.53 in the early 1970s and the population growth rate peaked a few years later at 2.97 per cent per annum.[21] Although IUDs were permitted starting in 1976, this was only in specific circumstances.

In 1990 the pro-natalist policy was abandoned, abortion was made legal and contraceptives began to be distributed through the health care system. Although the contraceptive use-rate remains low (particularly among men) fertility has declined rapidly. This is partly attributable to very high rates of abortion. There were 386.2 abortions per 1000 live births in 1990[22] and 445.4 per 1000 births during 1991.[23]

Fertility rates have declined from 7.49 in 1973, to 5.54 in 1983 to 3.84 in 1991, the most substantial reduction occurring among women between the ages of 35 and 49.[24] According to the Report on Population prepared for the Cairo Conference, fertility decline has occurred throughout the whole country, and in some provinces more than a 50 per cent reduction was observed.

It is quite clear that some part of the fertility decline in Mongolia is a long-term trend related to the deep socio-economic changes that the country has experienced during the past 70 years, involving substantial improvements in the standard of living of the population. However, as can be seen in Table 5.1, during the last few years there has been a remarkably steep decline in the birth rate, with a corresponding sharp fall in the population growth rate. This is clearly a result of economic distress and widespread poverty, with many women deciding to terminate pregnancies because of severe economic difficulties and uncertainty about their ability to feed and clothe another child.

Despite the falling birth rate and the low rate of growth of population which prevails at present, there is nevertheless a need for a population policy and a family planning programme in Mongolia, on grounds of extending women's choice and improving women's health, particularly for poor women whose health is at greater risk.

In addition, at present, 5.5 per cent of pregnancies are in women under 20 years and 10 per cent in women over 35 years of age,[25] which are high-risk ages for pregnancy. Maternal mortality among women

TABLE 5.1   Mongolia: crude birth rate, crude death rate, population growth
            rate and maternal mortality rate, 1989–93

	Crude birth rate	Crude death rate	Population growth rate (%)	Maternal mortality rate (per 10 000 live births)
1989	36.4	8.4	2.80	13.0
1990	35.3	8.5	2.68	12.0
1991	32.9	8.8	2.41	13.0
1992	29.1	8.4	2.07	20.0
1993	21.5	7.9	1.36	n/a

over 35 accounts for 31.5 per cent of the total MMR,[26] which itself
has risen sharply during the transition (see Table 5.1). In circumstances
of continued limited access to contraception, abortion, with its attend-
ant risks to women's health, is still the principal form of limiting family size. In 1990 there were 39 abortions for every 100 live births,
with around one abortion for every live birth for women over 35.[27]
The present level of contraceptive use among Mongolian women is
only 15 per cent. Therefore widespread access to safer means of contraception is a vital necessity.

The focus of population policy needs to shift towards extending
knowledge of, and access to contraception, to the population as a whole,
including men. Men's attitudes must also change so that they do not
resist, or in other ways impede, the practice of contraception. Too often,
the cultural norms of the male population are not taken into consideration and in the absence of efforts to address male cultural values, family-
planning programmes elsewhere have failed.

SUMMARY AND CONCLUSIONS

Mongolia's impressive health-care delivery system is in crisis, and
therefore the health status of the population is under some considerable
threat. The economic transition has resulted in decreases in funding
and critical shortages for the health sector. Maternal mortality, for
example, increased sharply in 1992, a trend which seems to have continued.

The priorities for health care seem to be clear. Maintaining the functioning of the primary health-care system, by reallocating resources

down the expenditure pyramid to *feldsher* and *sum* levels, and sustaining the routine preventive services for the entire population, are urgent necessities. Donor support in the form of equipment, including transport equipment, would be an important element in maintaining rural health care services, and in containing the increase in poverty.

In particular, the maternal and child health services should receive priority, with a restoration of previous high levels of contact with antenatal and hospital delivery services and improving the quality of services. In combination with the national family-planning programme, improved maternal health services can achieve lower maternal mortality rates. This would also require a combination of reallocation of national resources and donor support in the form of equipment.

Managerial capacity within the health sector at all levels needs to be strengthened, to enable health-sector decision-makers to allocate and utilise resources more efficiently, including the allocation of staff. This, too, is an area where donor support can make an important contribution.

Mongolia is now facing serious nutritional problems. Although there is now a system in place to monitor the nutritional status of children, no work has yet been done to assess the extent of poor nutrition or malnutrition among adults. The Ministry of Health needs to develop surveys for monitoring nutrition problems among vulnerable adult groups and to assist in designing appropriate interventions.

To reduce iron-deficiency anaemia, iron-folate supplementation should be made available in sufficient quantity to be supplied to all pregnant women.

The incidence of protein-energy malnutrition among children aged 13–24 months strongly suggests that a significant impact could be made by supporting correct breast-feeding practices. This could be effected by an educational campaign to promote correct breast-feeding.

The Ministry of Health needs to increase its efforts to improve the nutritional knowledge of health workers and parents. The Nutrition Research Centre should be involved in curriculum development for medical schools. Also, improvements in both content and message design are needed for an effective nutritional education campaign geared to parents.

Donor technical assistance will be required in the development of a nutritional curriculum in medical schools and in developing effective public nutritional education campaigns.

In the field of population policy, the Ministry of Health needs to increase the knowledge of women and men about family-planning methods. The goal of the jointly-sponsored MOH and UNFPA project to strengthen maternal and child health and family planning is that 80 per cent of men and women will be knowledgeable about at least three family-planning methods by 1996. Knowledge about the benefits of birth-spacing must also be improved.

Family-planning practice, as well as knowledge, has to shift away from abortion and to the use of safer methods. It is therefore imperative that access to effective contraception be provided and sustained, particularly in rural areas, through the existing primary health-care delivery system. In addition to an adequate supply of contraceptive devices, health workers, especially rural health workers, must be trained in their use and in how to handle side-effects or complications arising from their use. Health workers should also become more knowledgeable about sexually-transmitted diseases (STDs) and their prevention.

Donor assistance would be needed both in the form of capital and technical assistance. Capital assistance will be required to ensure an adequate supply of contraceptive devices for the immediate future, to be distributed through the existing health-care system. Technical assistance will be needed to provide training for health workers and to develop family-planning informational materials for public dissemination.

NOTES

1. See K. Griffin and T. McKinley, *Implementing a Human Development Strategy*, (London: Macmillan, 1994), pp. 45ff.
2. Ibid., p. 46.
3. See UNICEF, *The Situation of Children and Women in Mongolia,* Ulaanbaatar, December 1993, p. 14.
4. See Ministry of Health, *Mongolia: Health Sector Review*, Ulaanbaatar, July 1993, p. 28.
5. See Ministry of Health, op. cit., p. 12.
6. UNICEF, *Mongolia Annual Report on Country Situation*, 1991, Ulaanbaatar.
7. UNICEF, *Mongolia: Annual Report on Country Situation*, 1993, Ulaanbaatar.
8. Ministry of Health, op. cit., p. 16. See also D. Munhoo, 'Current Situation of Mongolian Women and their Goals in Near Future', Paper prepared for the National Seminar on Women's Issues, 1992, who states that, 'Rural women and low-income group women accounted for 83 per cent and 73.5 per cent of maternal deaths in 1992', p. 6.
9. See Ministry of Health, op. cit., Ch. 4.
10. Ministry of Health, op. cit.
11. Ministry of Health, op. cit., p. 63.

12. Ibid., p. 63.
13. Sara Randall, 'Issues in the Demography of Mongolian Nomadic Pastoralism', *Nomadic Peoples*, 1993, p. 217.
14. UNICEF, *The Situation of Children and Women in Mongolia*, Ulaanbaatar, 1993, p. 8.
15. UNICEF, *Mongolia: Child Nutrition Survey*, Ulaanbaatar, 1993, p. 9.
16. UNICEF, *The Situation of Children and Women in Mongolia*, Ulaanbaatar, 1993.
17. Ibid., p. 23.
18. UNICEF, *Mongolia: Child Nutrition Survey*, op. cit., p. 17.
19. Ibid.
20. Ibid., p. 18.
21. UNICEF, *The Situation of Children and Women in Mongolia*, 1993, Ulaanbaatar, p. 11.
22. Ibid., p. 11.
23. The National Preparatory Committee for the International Conference on Population and Development (ICPD), *Mongolian Country Report on Population and Development 1993*, Cairo, 1994, p. 8.
24. Ibid., p. 7.
25. Ministry of Health, *Mongolia: Health Sector Review*, Ulaanbaatar, 1993, p. 45.
26. Ibid.
27. Sara Randall, op. cit., p. 225.

6 Mongolian Women and Poverty During the Transition

Barbara Skapa

The spectacular achievements of three generations of Mongolian women under a pro-women socialist policy helped to transform Mongolia from a near-feudal autocracy to a modern state. The modernity achieved by women and the economic and social independence of the female half of the population is being severely undermined during the current period of transition to a market economy. The last few years have been characterised by a loss of well-being for almost all: loss of jobs for many and loss of the social support systems upon which the young and future generations depend. However, the transition has had a disproportionate effect on women: they have lost more jobs than men and they have even lost themselves to the rising trend of maternal mortality.

Because of the severe fall in incomes that has accompanied the economic reforms, Mongolian women have lost the strong social supports that released them from the domination of reproductive responsibilities. They have gained little in return as many spiral into poverty. Yet the current government, for the first time in two generations, has no policy on women. Despite this, most women are surviving and some are even prospering. They are leading the way for others to follow. Their efforts, supported by a vocal consortium of professional and unskilled women, hold promise.

The generous infrastructure that supported women in the former socialist economy is crumbling but has not disappeared. It is possible to rebuild it, and this infrastructure, combined with the collective and individual efforts of women coping with poverty, can be used as a foundation on which to construct a strategy that taps the human capital embodied in Mongolia's women.

This chapter is concerned with issues that affect women: we examine their historical achievements, the erosion of those achievements and the feminisation of poverty during the transition period, the responses by women to their poverty, and the response of government. Finally, we present proposals for restoring gender equity to a central feature of economic and political life, as in the past.

ACHIEVEMENTS BY AND FOR WOMEN: FROM FEUDALISM TO STATE-SPONSORED FEMINISM

The dynamics of gender equity in Mongolia can be characterised as a sequence of historical periods when equity was rapidly promoted after the 1921 Revolution, achieved spectacular results in the 1920s and 1930s, underwent a period of regression in the 1940s, was then re-promoted, and since 1989, has experienced a period of retrenchment. The dynamics have not been linear, but the results have been dramatic in a region of the world where women on the eve of the twenty-first century are still subordinated to men economically, socially and politically. In comparison to the female populations of developed countries, Mongolia can be justly proud of the achievements of its women and girls.

The active policy on women's development during the socialist period, and the generous support given to women's issues, have been undermined by the political changes that have swept across all the countries of the former Soviet bloc. Mongolian women are not alone in witnessing the collapse of the state-subsidised systems that allowed them to participate fully in the nation's economy in equal measure with men.

Well into the twentieth century, most Mongolian women existed on the margins of a feudal society whose social and economic parameters were dictated by a landed aristocracy and Lamaist theocracy. That period, under the Manchus, lasted about two centuries, prior to which women had considerably more equality with men. One of every four boys joined the Lamaist celibate monkhood: a practice that restrained Mongolia's fertility rate and in some measure alleviated extreme rural poverty. The status of women under feudalism radically changed during the 70 years of socialism. Following the 1921 Revolution, women rapidly achieved equal opportunity with men in education and employment. Women could and did dissolve marriages, confident in the knowledge that state-provided child-care services would ensure that their lives were not disrupted or their progress impeded.

During the 1930s enormous gains were made by and for women: 16 women were ministers, deputy ministers and agency heads, 35 per cent of judges were women, 50 per cent of people's assessors in lower and

TABLE 6.1   Gender indicators in Mongolia

Indicator	Circa 1970	Circa 1980	Most Recent
1. Total population (in thousands)	1248	1662	2250
2. Sex ratio (males per 100 females)	99.2	100.0	100.4
3. Population growth rate (per cent)	2.8	2.8	1.4
4. Population in broad age groups (per cent)			
Female			
0–14	43.0	42.2	40.5
15–49	46.0	44.9	47.5
50–64	7.6	8.3	7.5
65+	3.3	4.5	4.4
Male			
0–14	32.1	43.0	41.5
15–49	54.8	45.5	47.8
50–64	8.8	7.9	7.2
65+	4.3	3.6	3.6
5. Median age (years)			
Female	18.4	18.6	19.4
Male	17.7	18.2	18.9
6. Crude birth rate (per 1000 population)	40.2	38.0	21.5
7. Total fertility rate (births per woman)	5.9	7.5	3.4
8. Mean age of childbearing (years)	n.a.	29.3	29.0
9. Crude death rate (per 1000 population)	12.3	9.9	7.9
10. Life expectancy at birth (years)			
Female	58.3	62.8	67.7
Male	54.2	58.4	63.2
F/M ratio of life expectancy	1.08	1.07	1.07

aimag courts were women; 40 women headed cooperatives; 14 women (out of 33) were in the Hural in 1940.[1] The leap forward was followed by a withdrawal of women from economic and political life as a period of political repression began. Women suffered from political victimisation directly and indirectly: thousands of them were tried, many more continued life without husbands, brothers or fathers who were persecuted and imprisoned.[2]

The achievements of Mongolian women in the most recent decade have been economic and social; they have made less progress in the political or technocratic spheres, and the nation's leadership elite has become more male in composition. The political leadership is now entirely male. There is not one woman of ministerial or vice-ministerial rank today and only three members of the Hural are women. Educational achievements for both boys and girls were impressive. In 1923 Mongolia's first secondary school had only five female students. By 1928 there were 558 women in secondary school. When the first university started graduating students in the early 1940s, 2400 of them were female. By 1969 76 per cent of all women were literate and by 1989 the literacy rate for women had risen to 86 per cent. Educational achievements are also reflected in enrolments in higher education: women are 50 per cent of mathematics students, 63 per cent of trade and business students, 78 per cent in foreign languages, 73 per cent of medical students, and 76 per cent of pedagogical enrolments. At the college level, women constitute more than three-quarters of all enrolments (premed, pedagogy, business).

Women accounted for over half (51.5 per cent) of Mongolia's workforce in 1990. In the banking, health and education sectors they dominate (60–80 per cent). Women predominate in several sub-sectors, notably, communications, trade, technology, utility services, public canteens, and insurance.

THE EFFECT OF THE TRANSITION ON THE FEMINISATION OF POVERTY

Women have been adversely affected by the economic transition in two fundamental areas: loss of jobs and loss of social services that enabled them to participate fully in the labour market. The loss to Mongolia of its female human capital is enormous, as is the loss of women's voice.

Because of reduced access to formerly routine health care, the maternal mortality rate has risen sharply. Happily, the infant mortality rate appears to be declining slightly. Assisted and self-abortions – the contraceptives not of choice but of necessity – have increased dramatically and as a result, the birth rate has fallen equally dramatically, as we saw in Chapter 5. Rural women until recently had large families, encouraged by a former generously pro-natal policy. Now these women and low-income women in general are penalised because state revenues no longer permit subsidies to large families. More children are kept at home instead of at school, and as we saw in Chapter 4, school enrolments have dropped sharply.

The picture we have of female poverty in early 1994 is of a rapid slide from general and equitable well-being into severe dislocation. Over 54 per cent of the registered unemployed are women. These registers do not take into account the semi-employed, and do not include the 33 000 working mothers with large families forced into early retirement in 1991.[3] More women (62 000) than men are looking for work, but, according to some reports, fewer are finding work because male managers of privatised firms are reluctant to hire women of child-bearing age or women with children.[4]

The collapse of day-care, child-care and school services has put severe strains upon family life and this has resulted in increased divorce rates: 109 000 women were divorced by husbands in 1989–90. The average divorce rate now is 9.3 per cent. There is also a rising number of orphans and abandoned children.[5] It is likely that the rising divorce rate leads to an increase in the number of unreported female-headed households since housing allocations by family size are no longer operative. The formerly liberal state support for divorced women with children has collapsed.

Alcohol abuse by men has resulted in a rise in violence against women. There were 2243 cases in 1990, and almost 6000 in the first quarter of 1993 alone. Under-reporting is widely suspected.[6]

The former pro-natal policy which rewarded women with many children now penalises them. Fourteen per cent of those under the poverty-line in mid–1993 were elderly pensioners, mostly women; 72 per cent of single heads of households, mostly female, are below the official poverty-line. 36 800 households are female-headed: of these, 24 600 have women as the sole breadwinner with children under 16.

Young women seeking work, like young men, are finding the search for job security difficult. Young women can no longer count upon the maternal health-care and child-care supports their mothers took for granted. Already the privatised sector is reported to be turning away female job candidates of reproductive age. A few women have challenged this discrimination in the courts: none of the accused firms have been fined. Those without employment and a source of income are beginning to turn to prostitution, with its associated sexually-transmitted diseases and the potential spread of AIDS.

Privatisation in the livestock sector has had unintended consequences for women. Privatised herds are now mixed. Prior to privatisation, women worked primarily in single-species collective units as dairy maids. But mixed herds require more tending, and processing of animal products requires additional family labour. Because of this it is estimated that rural women now labour three hours more per day than men. They also sleep less than men, yet they still have to take care of cooking, cleaning, the elderly, children and the infirm.[7]

There is no official reporting of invisible female-headed households in rural areas, yet their experience is cause for alarm. These women's herds, which may barely survive from one severe winter into the next, cannot be adequately tended. To buy food, the women sell their animals to traders and with depleted animal resources, they eventually lose their independence and move back to their mothers' *gers*.[8] If they remain in their rural *gers* their futures are bleak: they may be forced to survive by working for richer neighbouring herders in exchange for food. These women usually are young, healthy, semi-skilled and with one or two very young children. Such women are slowly sinking into deep poverty.

An issue that has not yet been properly examined is how the legal framework affects women, and how legal issues could marginalise them further. Programmes intended to reduce rural poverty should carefully inspect the proposed Land Law which has a potential for discriminating against women in lease rights because of the (small) size of their herds.[9] An additional legal factor is the proposed Family Code Law which assures inheritance rights of animals, and possibly land-lease rights to boys, but not to girls, thereby further eroding the future economic status of women.[10]

Voice is critical to marginalised people in promoting and protecting their interests. Women have lost their voice since 1989. They wield less policy-making power than 50 years ago: only 11.7 per cent of the members of the Supreme Court are women, only 11 per cent of those in the diplomatic service are women and no woman is a governor of an *aimag*.

WOMEN'S RESPONSE TO THE TRANSITION

Women have not remained passive during the last four years of retrenchment. Two trends are emerging: female social and political activism and entry into the private sector.

As regards social and political action, women have created networks and interest groups to promote their interests. There are about eight formal women's non-governmental organisations in Ulaanbaatar and an unknown number of other groups scattered around the regional hospitals, Red Cross local councils, social services, schools and universities. Another network has emerged of expatriate feminists and field researchers, female and male, concerned with the deterioration of the standard of living of Mongolian women.

Other groups, such as the Mongolian Women's Federation, which was able to reach out and deliver services to the most remote regions of Mongolia, have emerged as non-governmental organisations with diminished state resources but increased foreign donor support. Since 1993 the non-governmental organisations and networks have organised themselves into a collective consortium called the Women's Consultative Group. Before the Consultative Group was established, a number of women in 1992 (who would later be among the founders of the Group) drafted a policy on women, at the President's invitation, for consideration by the government. Unfortunately, the proposed policy has languished for lack of response from the Hural. (This is discussed further below.)

The networks have had a broad agenda. The agenda includes equal access to work, equity in housing, legal issues and education, access of women to credit, generating employment, crisis intervention in health care for mothers and infants, promotion of the women's movement, formal and vocational education for girls and women, a clearing-house and an independent database.

Clearly most of these issues are responses to the deterioration of the status of women in Mongolia during the current economic crisis. In addition, some women's groups have expressed fears of indifference or hostility by government to women. The deterioration of women's status is primarily economic but it also has political dimensions, given the absence of government policy or machinery for women. Some of the issues (education, legal rights) have long-term implications for future employment opportunities of today's girls. Others have immediate implications, e.g. the survival of single-herder women and elderly women living alone.

It is likely that the conditions of very poor women with children and of elderly women on a fixed income will be the most difficult to ameliorate. These women will continue to need substantial assistance in the form of transfer payments.

In the private sector, in order to feed and protect their families, many women have taken risks and seized upon opportunities to become self-employed, to own and operate enterprises, to form the first associations of women in business.[11] Very few have received institutional support for their initiative: most are self-starters who still cope with the daily burdens of family life. These women are looked upon by others as role-models or mentors. Indeed some of them informally finance and assist others.

Women without small children often have entered the informal sector. They trade or barter in the hope of accumulating enough capital to establish formal sector businesses in production and service activities. This trend, if it continues, has a potential for generating employment for both women graduates and unemployed or semi-employed women. One donor, UNIFEM, has assisted this development by providing credit loans averaging $2000. The experience and success of that pilot effort holds promise for other similar schemes.

Examples of skills being turned into profit abound. Those who worked previously in defunct state-run canteens became at first street-peddlers of baked items, then private-canteen operators, then restaurant-owners, then mass-producers of bottled juices or pastries. A dentist opened a private dental clinic with the help of a small loan from a special credit line for women. A former state truck mechanic, out of work, received a loan and put herself and her brothers to work on repairing trucks. She now has a registered business and is looking for a tyre supplier and a larger workspace. An amateur photographer invested a small loan from her family and set herself up in business in her ground-floor apartment. A woman who once worked in a state meat factory started making sausages at home to peddle on the streets. Within six months she obtained a small loan under the UNIFEM project and repaid it with an additional contribution to the fund 'so that other women could profit'. A year later she leased production space, hired 14 employees from the factory where she once worked, and obtained good-quality used equipment from Germany which she financed with another loan. An educator has turned from teaching to printing textbooks. A hairdresser, operating out of her house, claims she has more customers than she can handle. The only constraint on expansion is the absence of a reliable supplier of beautycare products. Indeed many small businesses complain about difficulties with materials supply.

The World Bank estimates that there are approximately 30 000 self-employed informal sector operators. These include female cross-border and domestic traders. It appears, however, that the domestic trading sub-sector may be contracting, probably because of saturated demand and declining real incomes. A survey of informal and registered business-owners in Ulaanbaatar indicates that the sector attracts both men and women in their early middle age. Entry into the sector is easier for women who have grown-up children who have left home and have re-leased, say, one room of a flat that can be used to start a business (hairdressing, dressmaking).[12]

Informal financial markets are active in Mongolia. It is estimated that only 15 per cent of the currency circulates within the banking sector. In other words, Mongolia is essentially a cash economy. Marginalised by the formal banking sector, small businesses turn to family and money-lenders for credit.[13] The money-lender rate is not particularly high given the rate of inflation, and this suggests that the banking sector is inefficient and neglecting good lending opportunities in the small business sector.

The experience of the UNIFEM project, the only credit project in Mongolia targeted specifically at the newly-unemployed, has been very favourable and indicates there is scope for replication on a large scale. The project was designed by UNIFEM in response to the disproportionate rise in unemployment among women. It is a pilot small revolving credit line ($30 000) yet it has attracted so much attention that men also are applying for loans. Its methods of operation are simple yet efficient: partnered with a commercial bank committed to small-scale lending and a non-governmental organisation, the Mongolian Women's Federation, it grants loans at commercial rates to start up businesses. Its failure rate is tiny: 98 per cent of loans are repaid promptly, a performance that is comparable to repayment rates in other women's loan programmes in other developing and developed countries. The bank is pleased with the pilot scheme and claims it now prefers women clients because they are more reliable than men. The loans are to individuals, rather than to groups, and are primarily urban based (in Ulaanbaatar and Darkhan).

Group lending operations have been designed by the project and could be used for women in isolated areas where outreach and monitoring costs are high. The businesses financed vary widely and reflect the skills of the professional and semi-skilled women who have been thrown out of work during the transition and seek to form their own enterprises.

There are several lessons of this project for the design of poverty-alleviation programmes. First, the pilot credit project succeeded because the NGO had credibility with the government, was technically assisted during its growing stage by UNIFEM and others and responded to a real need with a practical immediate solution. Second, the role of government was minimal, not by intent, but *de facto*. The Ministry of

Population Policy and Labour, which authorised the project, has made little contribution to it. While the Mongolian Women's Federation kept the Ministry informed, the feedback from the project's achievements (employment generation in particular) into the design of policies for poverty alleviation has been weak. This raises questions about the capacity of the Ministry to manage a large-scale poverty programme.[14] Understaffed, under-equipped and operating with very limited guidelines, the Women's Affairs Desk at the Ministry finds it difficult to address the female half of Mongolia's economically active population.[15]

Third, credit projects for women succeed when the partner banks and the intermediary NGO both work in tandem: one bringing banking resources to the effort, the other its outreach and monitoring capacity. Fourth, and by no means unimportant, is the personal commitment of female banking staff and NGO staffers and volunteers to the effort: these represent an invisible asset of feminine solidarity and consciousness. The predominance of women in banking, combined with feminine solidarity, has been translated into extraordinary unrenumerated effort, such as visiting clients in their *gers* or apartments on foot or by bus, encouraging elderly women to manufacture items for sale, advising clients on alternative sources of raw materials, and providing psychological support. Fifth, the rate of job-creation under the revolving loan fund is much higher than usual: over 1000 jobs created in 110 new businesses. The women owners prefer to hire family members and trusted former co-workers from state enterprises. Most but not all employees are women.

THE RESPONSE OF GOVERNMENT TO WOMEN

The response of government to issues affecting women, as we have seen, has been halting. Mongolia's 1992 Constitution does guarantee equal rights for men and women 'in political, economic, social, cultural, and family life'. The Law on the Government has charged the government with elaborating state policies for children, youth, women and the elderly. This instruction remains unfulfilled in the case of women.

A policy drafted in 1992 by concerned women's groups, mentioned earlier, contains provisions for equal pay for equal work, the right to education, medical care, and ownership and inheritance of property and freedom of reproductive choice. The draft also proposes support of the women's movement and the activities of non-governmental organisations. It urges maintenance of child-care services. The draft also draws particular attention to the need for an economic policy for women; it proposes mechanisms for enlarged access to domestic and donor credit and technical assistance for promotion of women's employment and businesses.

The lack of policy affects line ministries (health, education, agriculture, population and labour) which are not given a framework in which to implement policies towards women and their children. The result is gender bias, whether intended or not. For example, the report of the Working Group on 'Rural Population Poverty Alleviation' cites statistics and proposes a number of measures to alleviate rural poverty, but it devotes no attention to female rural poverty. The problems of female-headed households are not discussed. While it refers to the paucity of health services and mentions 'sad cases when some young men's poor health condition does not allow them to serve' in the army, it fails to draw parallels with the health condition of young women. Clearly the Ministry of Population Policy and Labour is concerned about the poverty of all kinds for all people, but it has not so far demonstrated an ability to analyse gender issues or to develop strategies to assist women. In the absence of a coherent government policy and guidelines on women's issues, the outlook for gender sensitivity, government support and interventions in favour of females is not encouraging.

ELEMENTS OF A PROGRAMME PROPOSAL

One conclusion which emerges from the above analysis is that priority should be given to enable economically active women to protect their achievements and become integrated into the evolving labour markets. Unless appropriate policies are developed to achieve this, large investments in women's human resources will be lost and there will be a need for unacceptable and probably unavailable levels of direct transfer assistance. The structure of services created for the benefit of women by previous governments, although threatened, should be revitalised before it completely collapses.

Secondly, gender equity in social and economic life can be sustained only by enacting a government policy for women, creating the machinery needed for policy implementation and providing adequate resources.

A set of interventions intended specifically to alleviate women's poverty should be included within the framework of the government's Poverty Alleviation Programme. These interventions should be based on the strategies women are already spontaneously adopting and on the experience gained from existing pilot activities. The time-frame is the very short term: urgent action is needed rapidly to create jobs and income-earning opportunities. The activities should be regional in orientation rather than national. The core of the interventions should be the establishment of credit mechanisms for women in a variety of locations.

A workshop of women's NGOs and networks should be held as soon as possible to design and target interventions, preferably in the summer of 1995 when air and land travel from *aimags* to Ulaanbaatar is more reliable. UNDP should be asked to finance the cost of the workshop which is estimated to be about $10 000 for 50 participants from all 18 *aimags*.

The key proposal is to create a Women's Business Fund of $5 million to promote small business. The credit is intended to be disbursed rapidly in the form of short- to medium-term loans. This fund will require approximately $600 000 in counterpart contributions (staff, offices, overheads) and technical assistance to help establish the scheme.

Judging from current experience, one can anticipate that between 100 000 and 225 000 jobs would be created, assuming that between 10 000 and 22 500 borrowers each employ 10 persons, as is occurring under the UNIFEM programme.

In selecting regions in which to launch the start-up credit scheme, the possibility of rapidly multiplying the programme within an *aimag* should be given priority. We do not recommend that the programme be launched simultaneously in all 18 *aimags*. On the contrary, before participating in the programme it is important that the *aimag* governments and their partners at *sum* and *bag* levels should demonstrate an ability to use credit productively to generate employment for women and an ability to recover loans.

In other words, we recommend that *aimags* be encouraged to compete with each other for start-up credit funds by demonstrating capacity, efficiency and effort. The local effort would necessarily involve the local financial community, which would of course be held to high performance targets. The proposed scheme would provide an incentive to the local governments to seek out and develop partnerships with local women's networks and non-governmental organisations, thereby increasing the visibility of such groups in civil society in general and promoting the status of women in particular.

The participation of intermediary organisations in the programme – NGOs, private voluntary organisations, Red Cross, local networks of professional women – will require some financial support to cover their operating costs (outreach, information dissemination, monitoring, communication). This should be designed to be operationally sustainable by sharing the interest-rate margins among the intermediaries and the participating banks.

Investment in public works programmes (see Chapter 3) is complementary to the start-up credit scheme. Public works can be directed in part toward the rehabilitation of government-owned buildings to provide the multi-resource facilities that are needed particularly at *sum* and *bag* levels. The Mongolian Women's Federation's network of training centres could also be used. These Women's Development Centres could serve as day-care centres while women undergo credit preparation training; as mini-business incubators, especially if mentored by volunteer local businesswomen; as buying clubs for raw materials, secure storage facilities, or business information centres for the general public. The potential of such centres to serve the public is great, but the focus should be kept on employment generation and credit delivery and recovery.

The local Women's Development Centres can be staffed by gender-sensitive personnel, both men and women, seconded from local government on either a full- or part-time basis and can be considered as a counterpart contribution to the programme.

NOTES

1. The former Great Hural and Small Hural had 460 and 33 members respectively. These parliamentary bodies were reorganised into one Hural which now has 76 members.
2. O. Enhtuya, *Mongolian Women and Information*, Ulaanbaatar, 1993.
3. D. Munhoo, *Current Situation of Mongolian Women and Their Goal in the Near Future*, Ulaanbaatar, 1993.
4. Ibid.
5. Battungalag, *Family in Mongolia*, Ulaanbaatar, 1993.
6. Altantsetseg, Mongolian Women Lawyer's Association, *Legal Issues of Mongolian Women*, Ulaanbaatar, 1993.
7. Battungalag, op. cit.
8. L. Cooper, *Patterns of Mutual Assistance in the Mongolian Pastoral Economy*, PALD, 1994, and N. Gerelsuren, *Rural Development and Women's Issues*, Mongolian Women's Federation, 1993.
9. L. Cooper, ibid.
10. Altantsetseg, Mongolian Women Lawyer's Association, op. cit.
11. The Mongolian Association of Businesswomen, formed in 1992, has 3000

members among 18 *aimags*; other associations have formed since then that reflect specialisation among sectors and locations.

12. B. Skapa, *Survey of Small Businesses in Ulaanbaatar*, WIBI, 1994.
13. B. Skapa, ibid.
14. The Employment Generation Project of the Asian Development Bank is aimed at small businesses in Ulaanbaatar. The $3 million loan is to be executed by NGOs in partnership with three banks. The project is in the inception stage of implementation by the Ministry of Population Policy and Labour but the Ministry has not been able to amass the necessary human resources requested by the Bank in order to meet the Workplan. Delay is therefore likely.
15. In March 1994 the Ministry of Population Policy and Labour was asked to establish a Department for Youth: the department is staffed and charged with addressing the urgent employment needs of graduating and drop-out students.

7 Rural Development: The Livestock Sector

Jeremy Swift

The rural economy, and within the rural economy the livestock sector, is the key to economic growth and the reduction of poverty in Mongolia.

ECONOMIC TRANSFORMATION IN THE COUNTRYSIDE

Transformation of the rural sector from a command to a market system is underway. So far it has not gone well. The livestock sector has contracted in the last three years; livestock production and livestock producers have fared badly.

The livestock collectives or *negdels*, although part of an unsustainable economic system, did bring great economic and social benefits to herders: people were freed from dependence on feudal lords and monasteries, production was developed along specialised lines, produce was marketed and consumer goods bought, children went to school, and health was protected. Economic liberalisation, from the herders' perspective, has taken away most of these gains in return for an illusion of economic freedom.

One problem has been the sequence of reforms in the rural sector. A logical sequence would have restructured input and output marketing first, in order to provide incentives and channels for increased production; in fact, livestock and production assets were privatised first, and the *negdels* were dissolved. Production and marketing risk was transferred to herders, who responded with risk-avoiding measures such as diversifying their herds. Livestock markets slumped, offtake was reduced, and many herders retreated into self-provisioning.

Some households did well at privatisation and since, but others did not, and extreme rural wealth differentials have reappeared for the first time since the 1930s. Livestock and consumer goods marketing have declined; services are much reduced. Rural poverty has increased to levels unknown in the last half-century. Although some of the econ-

omic trends have been reversed, productivity and offtake in the livestock sector, and herding household welfare, are lower now than they
have been for decades.

The government places great hope on the livestock sector to lead
the recovery of domestic production and exports,[1] and thus to eliminate rural poverty.[2] For these hopes to be realised, substantial further
reforms and investments are needed in the livestock sector.

RURAL POVERTY

The scale of rural poverty is disputed. Some people claim that there is
no rural poverty, because 'rural people have animals and can live from
them', but this ignores the fact that many rural households have too
few animals, and that some households, like those headed by women
or the elderly, may not be able to balance labour and resources. An
estimate of the distribution of herd size by household is given in
Table 7.1. Inevitably it is general, putting together all animals without
consideration of species, and all households without consideration of
size. It suggests that 59 per cent of rural households have fewer than
50 animals, a figure often used as a poverty threshold by rural admin-
istrators, and that 19 per cent have fewer than 10 animals, which certainly amounts to extreme poverty.

The income measure of poverty, generally used in the urban sector,
is difficult to interpret in the rural economy where a large part of production is consumed within the household. It seems also that different

TABLE 7.1 Herd size distribution, 1992

Herd size (number of animals)	Households (percent of total)
< 10	19
11–30	23
31–50	17
51–100	22
101–200	14
201–500	5
> 500	negligible
Total	100

Source: A. Enkhamgalan, reported in Asian Development Bank, *Agricultural
Sector Survey of Mongolia*, Manila, 1994.

aimags calculate incomes and poverty thresholds in different ways. In Uvs each animal in the herd is attributed a standard annual income value, and the total herd added up to give a nominal income. In the mountain areas of Uvurkhangai, the poverty threshold is calculated at 21 *bod* per household;[3] in the Gobi areas of the same *aimag*, household herd-size is multiplied by standard production coefficients per animal, and the estimated production valued at current market prices, to give an estimated household income, which is then measured against the national minimum income level. In other *aimags* the estimate of the number of poor people is based mainly on the direct knowledge of local officials. Herders themselves have complex concepts of poverty, based primarily on animal holdings but including other assets and attributes deemed necessary for effective livestock production, the most important of which are sufficient household labour, skill and experience; the capacity to respond to increased market opportunity and assist those in need are also perceived as a part of wealth.[4]

There is a clear need for better and more disaggregated measures of rural poverty, based in part on local perceptions.

IMPORTANCE OF MACROECONOMIC AND INSTITUTIONAL FACTORS

This chapter deals with rural development, and focuses on institutional and micro-level issues. But little rural development can take place, however wise the decisions about the micro-economy, without solutions to macroeconomic problems. These include interest rates charged to rural borrowers (currently at 8 to 12 per cent per month), livestock:cereal and urban:rural terms of trade (currently very unfavourable to herders), and insufficient infrastructure. Development will only take place when these issues are resolved more favourably for rural producers. The macroeconomic reforms outlined in Chapter 1 are an essential part of a successful rural development strategy.

This chapter focuses mainly on institutional development – land tenure, organisations, markets, credit – in the rural sector. The main cause of stagnation in the rural economy is institutional shortcomings, and the answer is better institutional frameworks; only these can provide the incentives and structures through which investment and accumulation can take place by rural people themselves. Institutions are especially important for a development strategy with a poverty and gender focus. Institutional change has started, but has not yet gone far enough, and mistakes have been made. The measures discussed in this chapter are the necessary groundwork for rural development.

From an institutional point of view, the most important development issues in the livestock sector concern herder organisation, land tenure, marketing, credit, risk and how to raise productivity.

HERDER ORGANISATION

Rural organisation is central to a poverty strategy, since it determines the way natural resources are managed, livestock and other commodities are produced and marketed, and other economic and social needs are met. Rural people participate in economic, social and cultural life through formal and informal institutions, and these institutions can be friendly or unfriendly towards an anti-poverty strategy.

The task is to facilitate the rebuilding of a sense of community and a capacity for joint social and economic action at different levels in the social structure. This will involve a mix of formal and informal organisations.

The transition towards a market economy has been accompanied by a proliferation of formal rural institutions, and customary ones have survived. For the 40 years before 1990, the countryside was organised monolithically through agricultural (in reality pastoral) collectives – the *negdels* – and state farms. In parallel to the district–province–national hierarchy of the collectives were similar hierarchies of party and government. Unnoticed in this logical structure, many customary, pre-revolutionary, forms of organisation and resource use survived. When the dismantling of the old state apparatus started in 1990, the *negdels* evolved rapidly into a variety of institutional forms, and some underlying customary institutions re-emerged. As a result, there is now great diversity of institutional forms in the countryside. The discussion here focuses on those in the livestock sector. Those relevant to a poverty-oriented development strategy include customary organisations based on kinship or shared residence, formal non-governmental organisations such as the Red Cross, Buddhist monasteries, the Women's Federation and livestock companies, and formal government technical and administrative organisations at *bag*, *sum* and *aimag* level.

(i) Formal Sector Organisations

The *negdels* were economic organisations, each occupying a whole district. *Negdels* were organised internally into a descending hierarchy of brigades, work teams (at which level the main specialisation of production occurred) and base camps or *suurs*, the latter made up generally of one or two households. Economic decisions were made by the *negdel* in the light of production and marketing plans transmitted from Ulaanbaatar and the province, and inputs were made available in the same way; live animal and animal product quotas were fixed for each household by the *negdel*; most detailed pasture management decisions were made at brigade level; *suurs* made day-to-day management decisions only.

Decollectivisation started in 1991 with the gradual transfer of *negdel* assets – livestock, machinery, winter animal shelters – to the members. Each *negdel* was given considerable latitude in deciding how to carry this out, with the result that many intermediate forms of organisation and property-ownership appeared. Initially most *negdels* became joint stock companies, with some continued collective ownership of assets and some common economic planning at the district level.

Companies were designed to be an intermediate step on the way towards more fundamental privatisation. Quite rapidly, the shareholding companies divided further, into limited companies (distinguished from shareholder companies by a smaller minimum asset value), voluntary cooperatives (*horshoo*), or dissolved completely, leaving individual households as independent private operators. In addition to those resulting from the progressive fragmentation of the *negdels*, some new small *horshoo* were also formed by newly-independent households for specific tasks, including the purchase of lumpy assets, like tractors or trucks, which could not be bought by individuals; others were formed by herding households to carry out tasks better performed collectively, such as marketing, hay- and fodder-making, and the provision of transport. Usually such *horshoo* were created on the basis of existing informal groupings at the neighbourhood level. There are now estimated to be about 40 *horshoo* in the livestock and fodder sector, and 275 companies.

The success of many herding companies and *horshoo* is limited by current economic conditions and the few marketing opportunities at the level at which these small, often poorly financed, cooperatives can operate. They need management and in some cases technical training, finance and market identification, as well as improvements in infrastructure.

Companies and *horshoo* were created under the 1991 Law on Economic Entities. *Horshoo* generally have capital assets of less than 500 000 tugriks and companies more. The total of 315 companies and *horshoo*, comprising some 70–80 000 herding households, are grouped together in a National Union of Agricultural Cooperators, the successor organisation of the Supreme Council of *Negdels*; the members of this organisation are all in the livestock sector, but include groups with fodder production and other activities.

There are a further 70 000 herding families, scattered throughout the country, which are classified as private independent households; there is some tendency for them to be richer than the others, and perhaps to be clustered nearer to towns. These independent herders have an organisation, the Association of Private Herders, to protect their interests.

There are also about 200 agricultural sector *horshoo* and shareholding companies, mainly derived from the former state farms and involved in grain, vegetable and intensive livestock production, and agricultural services, which are organised into a separate association, the Union of Mongolian Production and Service Cooperatives. Other organisations responsible for processing rural products also belong to this Union. Almost the entire membership of this Union, totalling over 2000 organisations, is urban-based.

(ii) Customary Institutions

Mongolian herders, of course, have their own institutions, customary loose organisational structures or ways of doing things. Such institutions are often almost invisible to outsiders, who sometimes argue as a consequence that they are irrelevant or incapable. The term 'institutions' is used here in the sense of any regular pattern of 'norms and behaviours that persists by serving some socially valued purpose'.[5] Such institutions may not even be perceived by their participants as an organisational structure as such, merely a habitual way of doing things, although they may also be more formal, as in a set of customary rules about the use of a well in the Gobi. In a country as large and lightly settled and administered as Mongolia, such institutions are the essential matrix through which rural economic and social activity is organised. They overlap and coexist with the formal organisations responsible for rural administration and development.

Mearns[6] has shown how the main pastoral institutions, both formal and customary, have evolved from before the 1921 revolution to the present period of decollectivisation. There has been a remarkable continuity of institutions and organisations.

The *khot ail* camp and *neg nutgiinhan* neighbourhood are the two potentially important customary institutions for development purposes.

At the encampment level, groups of households organised themselves into *khot ail* camps before collectivisation as the basic unit of cooperation in production; during the collective period, such camps were abolished and the basic unit became a one- or two-household *suur*. However the *khot ails* reemerged rapidly, performing their previous economic and social functions, in response to the dissolution of the *negdels* in the early 1990s.

Khot ails are generally made up of between two and twelve households, who are often but not necessarily related by blood or marriage; they tend to be larger in ecologically productive areas, and smaller in more marginal areas. Households within a camp assist each other in production activities such as day-to-day herding, cutting wool and hair, making felt, moving camp and making hay. Each *khot ail* has an acknowledged leader who is generally the most experienced male herder. Although animals are normally milked individually in each household, camp herds may be grouped together by species, with each household taking it in turn to provide a herder. In addition to capturing economies of scale in herding, *khot ails* also have social and ritual functions.

Groups of *khot ails* using the same general area organise themselves informally to coordinate their use of pasture and hay-making land, water, and other natural resources, and to form search parties to look for lost animals. During hard winters or droughts, these *khot ails* tend to move as a group to a new pasture area. Such neighbourhood groups vary considerably in size (from 4 to perhaps 20 *khot ails*), and in the spatial area they occupy, depending on water availability, topography, forage yield and quality in different ecological zones. They are known generally as *neg nutgiinhan* or 'people of one place', with regional variants such as 'people of one valley' or 'people of one water source'. Very often such neighbourhood groups have a ritual point of focus, such as a shamanistic cairn or Buddhist temple, within their area. There is considerable regional variation in these neighbourhood groupings, which operate with different levels of organisation, detail and authority in different areas.

Neg nutgiinhan groups used to facilitate the coordination of grazing management and watering. These tasks were formalised during the *negdel* period by work teams and brigades, but the earlier loose territorial groupings have re-emerged following decollectivisation.

At the higher administrative level, there has been continuity with the recent past, and a new administrative level, the *bag*, has been added below that of the *sum*.

Customary institutions such as these are potentially important partners for development with government and national NGOs, and as independent organisations undertaking a variety of activities connected with resource use, economic production, marketing, and poverty alleviation. Neighbourhood groupings may be appropriate group-holders of pasture and water leases. *Khot ail* camps may be potential group credit-holders or provide the framework for primary human or animal health care.

The variety of Mongolian customary rural organisations provides a chance for innovative institution-building. Most development interventions in the pastoral sector, including poverty alleviation, require the involvement of groups of herders, not individual households. Such groupings already exist; they should be strengthened where appropriate, and their relationship to the formal institutions of modern government clarified and regularised. Because of their regional diversity, no general model can be proposed, but the approach which is proposed here is to work with such institutions as well as with the formal structures of government and the formal non-governmental organisations such as the Red Cross and the Mongolian Women's Federation. The variety of informal and formal institutions is one of the strengths of present rural organisation in Mongolia. A poverty-oriented programme should seek to strengthen aspects of these organisations, and work through them.

(iii) Policy Reforms

To achieve this, the following policy reforms are required:

Legal Status of Cooperative Unions. There is a need to clarify the legal status of the cooperative unions. The three national unions of herders, and especially the National Union of Agricultural Cooperators, which represents the largest number of herder groups, are nominally independent of government but are in fact subject to a variety of constraints. They function at present under the law governing NGOs, but are often required to function as though they were economic entities. Government takes a hand in the nomination of local staff. There are two new laws in preparation, one on *horshoos*, the other on companies, which would resolve some of these problems. These laws should be finalised and presented to Parliament for approval as soon as possible.

Role of Cooperative Unions. The cooperative unions need to be given a decision-making role at central and local level. The cooperative unions (together with the Association of Private Herders) represent in theory all Mongolian herders. As such they should be represented at key points in the decision-making process concerned with rural development and with poverty alleviation. This includes the National Council for Poverty Alleviation, and the *aimag* poverty-alleviation councils.

Customary Groupings.   Customary groupings should be recognised as potential legal entities and development partners. As discussed below, group leases are the best institutional solution for some pasture- and water-resource tenure, and customary user groups, usually at the neighbourhood or *bag* level, are the most appropriate group to hold such leases. Customary groups, such as *khot ails*, may also be appropriate institutions for some types of group lending arrangements, as well as offering an organisational framework for activities such as education or primary health and veterinary care. Such groups are now the first line of support to poor households in event of accident or need. At present there is no way such groups can be formally constituted for development purposes, other than to be created into *horshoo* cooperatives, which are recognised in the Law on Economic Entities. There is a need for further research and discussion in the countryside on how best to achieve this, and then to draft appropriate legislation. There is also a need to think creatively about how such informal groupings can be helped to extend their support to poor households or those who suffer personal disasters; subsidies on group grazing-fees or insurance premiums and reductions in animal taxes might be used to encourage such intra-group cooperation.

(iv) Technical Assistance

Technical advice is needed in three priority areas:

Customary Institutions.   Further research is needed to identify the full range of variation in customary institutions, and how these can best be given sufficiently formal status, or incorporated into formal sector organisations, to be able to act as development organisations; the tasks where this might be appropriate include holding pasture leases, managing group access to credit, and identifying and acting on poverty. An important objective is to ensure that the interests of poor households and those headed by women are protected during this process of formalisation. This work should build on research already carried out by the Mongolian research institutes, especially those of Geography and Geocryology, Agricultural Economics, Animal Husbandry and Land Policy. This is discussed in greater detail in the section on land tenure below. This work should be coordinated with comparable work planned by DANIDA on pastoral organisations, although this is mainly concerned with members of the Association of Private Herders.

Credit and Other Financial Services. A prime need in the herding economy, especially in the context of poverty, is for credit for restocking, for livestock marketing, and for other economic activities. Technical assistance is needed to identify, first, the appropriate channels through which such credit can be extended to herders (including perhaps the Agricultural Bank and the Mongol Horshoo Bank), and as importantly, how herders can best be organised to make good use of credit. Customary groupings, formalised in some manner to be determined, taking group loans for allocation to member households, may be one solution, but the feasibility of this needs to be examined in some detail, since it would be a radical departure in Mongolian credit experience. Group lending arrangements to companies would, on the other hand, be immediately feasible. Credit is discussed in greater detail later in this chapter.

Small Enterprise Promotion. Herder groups, formal or informal, are in a good position to exploit possibilities for small enterprise development, ranging from local manufacture of items of everyday use in the pastoral economy (such as clothes, saddles or household items), through simple processing of animal products (such as washing wool, processing milk, leather-preparation), to setting up major marketing enterprises (such as national or international marketing of live animals). Technical assistance is needed to identify particular small-enterprise opportunities to be carried out through one of the Unions of Cooperatives in cooperation with other NGOs.

PASTURE-LAND TENURE

Common grazing land makes up 79 per cent of all land in Mongolia and its sound management is a critical component of a poverty-oriented rural development strategy. Unambiguous and secure tenure is an essential prerequisite for poor households to produce more, and this is especially important in a nomadic pastoral economy.

A new Land Law is at present before Parliament, and its enactment will set the framework for future land-allocation and management decisions. This section, based mainly on the conclusions of a recent detailed study of pasture land tenure options,[7] outlines key issues in this respect.

(i) Customary Tenure

Most livestock production in Mongolia depends on natural pasture, which is driven principally by low and variable rainfall. Because of the low productivity and inter-seasonal and inter-annual variability of plant production, pastures can rarely be divided between households as private individual grazing lots. Viable pastoral territories must include pastures for all four seasons, and for a range of wet and dry years, and so must usually be quite large, although they vary considerably according to local ecological conditions; such territories generally increase in size as mean annual rainfall diminishes and variability increases. Territories range in size from 100 to 200 sq. km. in productive mountain valleys to several thousand sq. km. in the Gobi.

Mongolian herding communities are generally organised around the management of these grazing territories. Customary grazing and water rights have evolved as a set of social customs regulating behaviour within and between such groups, including informal mechanisms to allocate pastures to households, to monitor and enforce compliance, and to resolve conflicts. These customary land-tenure arrangements within and between neighbourhood groups of different sizes continued to a large degree through the period of collectivisation. They continue to work well most of the time now but cannot cope with the pressures of privatisation unless new, formal (i.e. laid down in written law) systems of land tenure are adopted which support and extend them. This process is under way with the draft Land Law before Parliament.

(ii) Grazing Tenure Reforms

Grazing land tenure reform should be guided by three main objectives:

 (i) *improved economic efficiency*, i.e. using land resources in ways which optimise productivity in the context of a particular set of production goals and constraints;
 (ii) *social justice and equity*, i.e. provision of a fair distribution of the benefits of production, and guaranteeing access to basic production resources, especially to poor households and those headed by women;
 (iii) *environmental sustainability*, i.e. not allowing present uses to reduce future productivity of the resource.

These objectives are closely interrelated. They may sometimes conflict, but more often support each other. It is important to stress that guaranteeing poor households land-tenure rights is not only a question of social justice – objective (ii) – but also contributes to improved economic efficiency – objective (i) – and also contributes to environmental sustainability – objective (iii) – since households with access to adequate pasture and adequate herds will use the land in more productive and sustainable ways than poor and deprived households.

There are several important problems to be faced in designing a new grazing tenure system. There have been changes in the distribution of livestock, especially greater concentration of livestock around *sum* centres and the main towns, and an increase in the number of herding households, especially new and inexperienced households who are not well-integrated into existing herding communities and may be unwilling to follow customary grazing rules; there has also been an increase in absentee herd-ownership which creates problems of conflicting animal management strategies.

In many countries land-titling – the process of registering and certifying existing informal or formal rights in land – is considered necessary to increase tenure security, as well as to provide collateral for credit and encourage land markets. However, tenure security can be achieved in Mongolian conditions by a process less demanding than full land-titling, and especially by strengthening existing informal tenure rights at the level of herder groups, by registering grazing-land title to such groups. Grazing-land title is not, under Mongolian conditions, needed as security for credit (herds can play this role), and title should not be used as a basis for creation of a market in grazing land, since this would encourage the privatisation and sale of the highest productivity pieces of land, without which the rest of the grazing system cannot be productive or sustainable. Such a process of strengthening existing informal rights must protect the rights of poor and marginal households, including especially woman-headed households; however it is no less effective at this than formal titling, and may indeed be more so.

The variety of Mongolian pastoral land tenure situations points to the need for a flexible range of tenure solutions which differentiates between different categories of pastoral resource:

- *point resources*, such as winter shelters and small wells, should in general be held as private individual freehold property or on individual leases from the state; in both cases the property should be heritable or transferable within families, but not saleable;
- *small-scale resources*, such as land around winter shelters, intermediate capacity wells, and arable and hay fields opened and cultivated by individual households, should in general be held on individual

leasehold from the state; in some areas, winter–spring pastures are also sufficiently distinct to justify individual state leases;

- *large-scale resources*, such as summer and autumn pastures, large-capacity wells, and arable and hay land opened and cultivated by groups (such as former brigades, *negdels* and state farms, companies and other economic entities), should be held as a group leasehold from the state. Where identifiable community groups such as well or valley groups exist at the appropriate level, they should be the leaseholder, constituted for this purpose as *horshoo* cooperatives. Where such customary groups do not exist, it may be necessary to encourage the creation of new economic entities at *bag* level to act as grazing-land leaseholders. Group leases would be an innovation in the formal system, but would correspond well to customary practice. Leaseholding groups should where possible be based on existing neighbourhood groups which already manage such resources. Most such leases should be issued on a rolling (i.e. regularly renewable well before expiry) basis for 30 to 40 years, subject to a satisfactory review of the performance of the leaseholder in keeping the conditions of the lease. Payment for leases should cover the administrative costs of registration, with grazing fees, discussed below, as the main source of revenue from pasture land.

Within all such new leasehold tenure systems, groups should be encouraged to make agreements on reciprocal access with neighbouring groups in exceptionally bad years, when the resources within the leased area are insufficient, or in cases where grazing resources are habitually shared by two or more leaseholder groups.

The draft Land Law can accommodate these proposed changes with minor modifications which could be introduced during its current passage through Parliament. The law should provide only a broad legal framework for the pasture tenure system; a new Land Policy is also needed to give detailed guidance on how the proposed new grazing tenure arrangements should be implemented.

Grazing-land fees have been debated for some time in Mongolia, and considerable research has been done by Mongolian institutions to provide a basis for calculating such fees. The objective of such fees is to formalise property rights in land, to encourage land users to manage land in a conservative manner, and to raise government revenue. Grazing fees are politically controversial in Mongolia, especially among herders, and their introduction needs to be done with extreme care, in ways which maximise perceived benefits to local herders.

Grazing fees will contribute towards the first objective if they are assessed on the territories leased by groups as a whole, and raised and paid by the group leaseholder. The group itself can then decide the allocation of the fee between its members in ways which protect the position and grazing rights of poor households. In order to achieve the objective of pasture-land conservation, the livestock head tax portion of the fee should be graduated with tax per animal increasing as herd size increases; land of higher quality and land close to *sum* centres should be taxed substantially more than land of lower quality or farther away from urban centres. There may also be a case for higher taxes on higher productivity animals than on indigenous Mongolian breeds, although this would be hard to assess and collect.

Revenue from grazing fees should contribute towards the cost of administering the system of land management and protection. If more substantial fees are raised, a significant portion should be paid into a local (*bag* or *sum*) fund for livestock development, including especially a new emergency fodder fund to protect herders during emergencies. Such a fund might also contribute towards the recurrent costs of *bag*- or *sum*-level services. Such locally visible uses would facilitate the introduction of fees. Grazing fees should not be seen as an important additional source of central government income.

MARKETING

An efficient marketing system for agricultural products and inputs is an essential component of a poverty-oriented rural development strategy. In Mongolia, this means principally livestock and livestock-product marketing. This section of the chapter, based on a recent detailed study of livestock marketing,[8] analyses this sector.

Livestock marketing, like production, is strongly seasonal in Mongolia. There is a slaughter season in late autumn and early winter: the animals are fat after the summer and early autumn peak pasture season, the end of the breeding season simplifies the selection of slaughter animals, protein is needed to replace diminishing milk supplies, and freezing winter temperatures makes refrigeration of meat unnecessary. Under the command economy, State Procurement Orders for live animals and products were met by producers in the pastoral collectives and state farms. Live animals were delivered by producers in early summer, trekked to the main urban consumption centres over the summer months, during which they put on weight, then slaughtered for domestic consumption or export; in addition, animals were exported live directly to Russia from border regions.

Other livestock products are also strongly seasonal. Milk and milk products are most available during summer and early autumn but, because of storage difficulties, not at other times of year. Wool, cashmere and other products are also harvested to a pronounced seasonal pattern, with animal wool and hair products marketed in spring and early summer, and skins and hides sold mainly after slaughter in early winter.

(i) Market Liberalisation

Liberalisation of livestock marketing has consisted mainly in the reorganisation and part-privatisation of the state marketing agencies, and the legalisation of private trade. A branch of the old Department of Trade and Procurement was privatised and set up as a Union of shareholder Consumer Cooperatives (CC), which compete in private markets as well as meeting residual state procurement orders for animals and livestock products. An Agricultural Commodities Exchange (ACE) was set up in 1991 as a joint-stock company to trade in agricultural commodities; it has a network of brokers at national, provincial and district level who buy livestock and their products on commission, and also help meet state orders. Other parastatal organisations in the livestock sector include Makhimpex (an Ulaanbaatar-based slaughter, meat-processing and trading company), slaughterhouses in Darkhan and Choibalsan, and several wool-trading and manufacturing concerns.

These parastatal enterprises benefited from the initial transfer of assets, and continue to benefit from government support, through the provision of subsidised credit and privileged access to essential inputs such as petrol. They are also burdened with continued state obligations. By mid-1993 state orders had officially been eliminated on all agricultural commodities except meat, where they had been replaced by a 'production capability plan', based on a comprehensive inventory of Mongolian livestock, through which central government fixed livestock marketing targets for each *aimag*, which were then negotiated at successively lower levels. The exact legal status of these targets is unclear, and they are met unevenly and unwillingly by herders and companies.

Exports of live animals and meat remain a near-monopoly of government through the parastatals (because of the strategic importance of the livestock barter trade with Russia, the main market), while exports of other animal products have been freed of restrictions, although an export ban on raw cashmere was reimposed in April 1994.

Private livestock traders began to operate in 1992 and their numbers have grown slowly since. They tend to work in more accessible areas, because of transport and communication difficulties; local government discriminates against them by reserving petrol for parastatal enterprises. Because of shortage of cash and consumption goods in the countryside, private traders usually operate on a partial barter system. However, because of the constraints imposed on parastatals by government, private traders are usually able to offer better prices to herders, and as a result are preferred by the latter. Private traders are active in export of livestock products, although they are not allowed to export live animals, meat or cashmere.

In summary, the liberalisation of livestock marketing since 1990 has had mixed results so far, and the situation is confused. The state's share of livestock trading has declined substantially, but remains significant, at about one-sixth of total offtake.[9] Shareholding enterprises in agricultural marketing have been set up, although government retains a substantial holding in the main ones. Such enterprises have benefited from the transfer of public assets and continue to benefit from subsidised credit, as well as privileged access to scarce inputs such as petrol. But they are also supposed to meet residual state requests for live animals, meat and other products, the legal status of which is unclear. Private traders are able to operate in most areas of livestock marketing, but are hampered by lack of access to inputs, including petrol and credit at economically viable rates. Exports of live animals and meat remain under government control; other exports, except raw cashmere, are currently free, although the administrative processes involved in export remain cumbersome and time-consuming.

The terms of trade have moved substantially against livestock producers,[10] and because of this, the marketing situation facing livestock producers has deteriorated dramatically. Prices for their products, especially live animals and meat, have stagnated, while prices of the essential foods they buy have risen sharply. Marketing channels are in disarray, and in most places producers are faced by only one or two buyers for any particular product, and no real competition. The most basic food staples, like flour and sugar, are sometimes unavailable to herders, reducing their incentive to market their animals, although this situation is now improving. There is little cash circulating in the countryside, and most marketing transactions are either on a deferred payment or barter basis, which further reduces producers' choice and flexibility.

The results were predictable. Marketed livestock numbers have fallen substantially. In parts of the countryside, there has been a retreat towards self-provisioning, with herders greatly reducing consumption of purchased foods like flour, and relying instead on increased meat and milk consumption from their own production.[11] Poor households have suffered particularly directly from these market imperfections, since they have less flexibility in marketing than richer ones. The contraction of livestock marketing – the most important rural economic activity – has had ripple effects throughout the national economy.

These changes have been damaging for herding households, especially poor ones. Surveys conducted during 1993–94 show:[12] (i) pastoral households are where possible meeting their consumption requirements from their own livestock production, with little involvement in the market; (ii) households prefer to sell animal products rather than live animals; (iii) where animal sales are necessary, middle-wealth households sell most. Rich households can meet more of their consumption needs through home consumption and sale of animal products. Poor households have few animals to sell, and have to meet their consumption requirements in other ways, including especially salaried labour where it is available, and work remunerated in kind, such as herding for richer households.

(ii) Marketing Reforms

Our analysis underlines the urgency of continuing policy reforms in livestock marketing. Initial sector reforms were based on the following principles:[13]

- continuing privatisation and building competition in the food and agriculture sector, and correction of mistakes made so far;
- liberalisation of farm-gate prices;
- infrastructure development;
- expanded production for export;
- a continuing role for the state in high-technology agriculture, including cereal production and mechanised dairy operations;
- continuing subsidised low-interest credit to ensure meat and cereals to meet state central requirements;
- a change from state procurement orders for urban meat supplies to a system of direct agreements between consumers and suppliers;
- creation of new livestock markets in the major cities;
- development of mobile butter production units by privatisation of former *negdel* butter-processing plants.

So far these guidelines have not all been successfully followed. The expansion of livestock marketing is an important component of a poverty-oriented development strategy for Mongolia. A good start has been made on reform. But inconsistencies remain in the policies, and in many cases policies have not been implemented effectively. The reforms have also been out of sequence: livestock marketing reforms should have been well underway before the start of reforms in production, so that the newly privatised production sector would have had market incentives to respond to.

Export limitations are a particular problem. The government has maintained or reinstated some export bans or restricted exports to parastatals on the grounds that the exports are of strategic importance (live animals to Russia), or in order to protect infant industries (cashmere). Although there may be some justification for both arguments, the losers in each case are the herders who, because of the limitations, receive a lower price for their products than they otherwise would. In addition, distortions are maintained in the structure of trading and the signals that are transmitted to the production system. If the government wishes to pursue such policies in the national interest, it must ensure, first, that herders do not lose, but are compensated for the losses they suffer, and second, that any such limits on trade last no longer than is necessary to meet their objectives: continually protected infant industries never grow up.

To complete the market reform process started in 1991, and to provide the stimulus to increased production, further policy reforms are essential. These are:

Remove Remaining Price Controls.   The government should allow meat prices to be determined by the market by removing the remaining price controls on meat, and by ending the system of procurement through *aimag* and *sum* level 'production capability plans' as well as price-fixing by city councils at the main slaughterhouses. State institutions (army, police, hospitals) should be supplied through the market. The losers from this move, especially the urban poor, should if necessary be compensated through a targeted income transfer or social security payments.

Create conditions for competition in marketing.   Conditions for equal access to livestock markets and free competition by all players should be created by the following measures:

• operating and investment credit should be made available on the same conditions to all operators in the livestock market, based only on demonstrated ability and creditworthiness; this should apply to parastatals, private-sector organisations (companies, *horshoo*, trading partnerships) or private individuals, who should compete for credit on an equal footing;

• livestock should be accepted as collateral for loans for livestock trading, as well as other purposes;

• the status of the Consumer Cooperatives and other parastatals such as Makhimpex should be redefined so as to remove the obligation to meet residual state orders, and to allow them to compete freely in the market;

• equal access to petrol, transport and other inputs should be guaranteed to different categories of trading organisation and individual traders;

• other advantages of parastatals in livestock trading should be removed, as should any state obligations on them;

• private traders should be permitted to enter the market for the export of live animals on the same terms as parastatals; export procedures should be simplified for all operators;

• the recent ban on the export of raw cashmere should be considered at best a temporary measure to allow the domestic cashmere processing industry to develop, protected from foreign competition; however, cashmere producers should be compensated for their loss of revenue, through a sales tax, so the burden falls on consumers;

• export quotas for meat and livestock products should be replaced by export taxes applied equally to all operators.

• the flow of information about prices and market opportunities should be improved at *aimag*, *sum* and company level, as well as by more detailed radio programmes at times herders can hear them.

Rehabilitate the Trekking System.   An efficient system of trekking livestock from throughout the country to the main consumer centres in the cities was developed during the command economy period. This included provision of fodder at fodder-farms on route, and the coordination of arrival dates at the slaughterhouses. The system has continued on a reduced scale since liberalisation, with private trekkers moving animals alongside the animals being moved under contract to the parastatals. The trekking system will remain necessary for the foreseeable future, and should be rehabilitated, with equal facilities for private traders and trekking agents. Land-tenure formalisation should ensure that the major trekking routes are given an adequate legal status. Private fodder enterprises should be encouraged to site themselves close to such routes and to the urban termini.

Infrastructure and Communications.   Market efficiency is constrained by inadequate present infrastructure and communications.

- investment in roads and public transport is a priority; marketplace infrastructure needs development in provincial centres; both of these are discussed in Chapter 3;
- market information is at present provided by the Agricultural Commodities Exchange, but their withdrawal from direct livestock trading in many places is likely to reduce the accuracy and timeliness of the information; maintaining and improving this service is important. Proposals are made elsewhere in this chapter about strengthening the *aimag*-level information exchange about livestock and other prices.

Decentralised administration.   Export of increasing numbers of animals to Russia and skins to China directly from regional centres requires that the administrative and veterinary health measures needed for such exports can be carried out in appropriate regional centres: Ulgii, Uliasty, Sainshand, Dalanzadgad, Darkhan, Choybalsan, Ulaangom, Moron, Khovd, Sukhbaatar.

Local processing.   Local processing facilities need to be developed to add value to raw livestock products for local consumption and for export.

Quality control.   There is a need to restore and develop quality control and grading of rural products in processing and marketing; ways need to be found to do this through the private sector rather than through the government.

CREDIT

Credit can play a key role in a poverty-oriented rural development strategy. But there are important constraints. There is almost no experience of credit among ordinary herders. Credit was not available within the command economy, and high interest rates since liberalisation started have discouraged herders from experimenting. Credit is little discussed among herders, who have no clear conception of what credit is or can do. Similarly, the banks have no experience of lending to herders. Therefore credit proposals should be designed with extreme caution, and include a long introduction period, and familiarisation and training on both sides.

With this proviso, two credit issues could be of particular importance to the livestock economy:

(i) **Restocking Poor Herders**

Privatisation of livestock ownership and other changes accompanying economic liberalisation have resulted in rapidly increasing inequality of livestock holdings between herding households, and the emergence, for the first time for several decades, of households with herd-sizes below the level considered necessary for an independent economic existence. In addition to equity considerations, this is also economically inefficient. Herding labour is characterised by substantial diseconomies of small-scale: for most herding operations (watering at manual wells and milking are exceptions), one full-time herder is needed for a flock of sheep whether there are 20 or 100, but labour productivity in the latter case is several times that of the former.

Small herds also have an impact on offtake rates and marketing. Poor herders sell few animals because they have few to sell. Animal sales-rates tend to rise as household herd holdings rise, then fall again as households become rich enough to live mainly from their own livestock products. When poor households move into the middle-wealth category, their offtake rates increase substantially, leading to increases in trade and benefits to urban consumers.

Policies to restock poor herders are therefore in the general economic interest, as well as meeting the objectives of an anti-poverty strategy. The animals used for restocking should be locally purchased, so there is no net increase in grazing pressure, but merely a redistribution of ownership. Indeed, since viable medium-sized herds tend to be managed better than very large ones, a redistribution of ownership will often lead to better environmental use.

The transaction costs of restocking programmes, especially those with complex repayment demands, tend to be high. In order to have a programme with low management costs and high social and economic impact, restocking should be carried out through the livestock companies or local customary groupings. The mechanism proposed is for credit to be made available to the companies to purchase animals and to lease them to herding households whose herd is below the locally agreed viable minimum (which will vary according to locality and predominant species).

The lease would take the form of a contract between household and company, under which the company would receive annual quotas of animal products in recompense for the cost of administering the lease, while the household keeps all the offspring. The number of animals leased should be calculated so that normal herd-growth over a period of three to five years, in addition to any animals already owned by the household, will take the household herd above the agreed local minimum. Independent private herders would be eligible for the same contracts through companies or through the local organisation of private herders. All leased animals should be insured by the company against unavoidable loss (especially snow, hail, drought) but not negligence (including accidents, wolf attack, etc.).

(ii) Development of Small Rural Enterprises and Marketing

Small rural enterprises, including marketing, are currently hampered by the lack of operating capital, spare parts and access to inputs. A further credit window should be made available to companies, *horshoo* and private individuals and traders for such small-enterprise development, including dairying, wool-washing, cashmere-combing, felt-making, clothes and shoe-making, vegetable- and fodder-cultivation and storage, transport and trading. Local comparative advantage would be an important principle, in order to diversify product lines and encourage inter-company trading.

In the Gobi there is a particular need to set up small well-repair and maintenance enterprises, to take in hand the many wells which have broken down through lack of spare parts or maintenance. There may be a role for credit in creating such enterprises. Clarification of the tenure status of such wells would be necessary before repair.

Training needs to be made available in small-business administration, accounting and enterprise management, so that groups and individuals can take advantage of credit. At *aimag* level, it is proposed that a business consultancy be set up to advise companies and individuals on the preparation of business plans, as well as undertaking market analysis and exchanging price information.

The Agricultural Bank, which is represented in all *sums*, is the natural organisation for the management of the credit funds described in the preceding paragraphs. However, the Bank has little experience of lending to herders, who are said to be net depositors to the system. The Bank does in principle accept livestock and personal valuables as collateral for loans. At present it is unlikely that the Bank could satisfactorily manage credit schemes on the scale needed, although a forthcoming Asian Development Bank training programme should improve this situation.

The major blockage to the implementation of credit programmes at market rates is the very high real rates of interest that currently prevail, which make loans for ordinary rural productive, manufacturing and trading activities impossibly expensive. If these macro-economic issues cannot be resolved, it will be necessary for donor-funded projects to manage credit funds directly in order to avoid creating precedents at commercial banks for heavily-subsidised rural credit.

RISK, ASSURANCE AND SAFETY-NETS

Mongolia, like other pastoral environments, is inherently risky for rural producers.[14] Risks come from the natural environment (particularly frozen snow cover – the most feared calamity – but also hail and drought), from animal disease, and latterly from the economic and political environment. Such risks are an important potential cause of extreme poverty and destitution. Under collectivisation, the formal redistributive mechanisms and virtually nation-wide pooling of risk, inherent in the socialist idea of the country as a single economic firm, proved effective in reducing risks to individual households. However, the transition to a market economy raises important questions about the division of responsibilities for risk-management between state and individuals. The terrible *dzuud*, or frozen snow cover, that affected three provinces in central western Mongolia in spring 1993, killing over three-quarters of a million animals, is a reminder that a poverty strategy has to cope with periodic major external shocks to the economic system.[15]

Risks of this sort can be divided into two categories: those that affect individual households at random in a herding community, and those that are community-wide; we call the first 'individual' risks, and the second 'covariate' risks.

In general terms, households within functioning local communities can without too much difficulty engage in strategies which minimise the impact of risks that do materialise. This is achieved by pooling risk among several households through mutual assistance or reciprocal action arrangements, or by spreading risk among activities within a household by diversifying sources of income (e.g. by herd-diversification or engaging in trading).

Where shocks affect all members of a community ('covariate' risks) such strategies cannot be sufficient: one household cannot help another, since all face the same problem. Similarly, risk-spreading within a household will be ineffective if the shock affects all sources of income simultaneously. Some larger institution than the community needs to intervene to provide insurance for this eventuality. In Mongolia at the present stage of economic development it would be foolhardy to suppose that private insurance markets are likely to cope adequately with such covariate risk, although they certainly have a role to play; the main responsibility must be undertaken by government.

(i) Individual Household Risk

Individual household risk has been handled in the past, and continues to be handled, in the first place by kin and neighbour assistance. Such assistance is not limited to risk-protection, but covers the whole range of needs arising from poverty, distress and danger, including care for orphans, the sick and old people, and helping poor households with food, animals and labour at peak periods. This local assistance has in the past been backed up by the dominant rural economic institutions: the feudal *hushuu* and monasteries before the revolution, and the *negdel* afterwards. The existence of strong formal rural institutions of this latter sort, providing a minimum safety-net for rural people, distinguishes Mongolia from other extensive pastoral economies facing the same sorts of risk, and may have contributed to a weakening of informal mutual assistance networks,[16] although the latter continue, in 1994, to provide the first line of assistance to households in trouble.[17]

(ii) Covariate Risk

The main risks facing Mongolian herding households, in order of decreasing importance as perceived by herders, are: extreme winter conditions, drought, animal disease, flash flooding, market failure and livestock predation.[18] In terms of the classification used earlier, extreme winter and drought conditions, and market failure are mainly covariate risks, the others mainly individual. Of these, extreme winter conditions (*dzuud*) are perceived by herders as the most dangerous risk they face, and are the cause of vary large-scale livestock deaths. Poor households are especially vulnerable to these disasters.

A chronology of major national *dzuud*s, from historical records and oral history, suggests that they have occurred at an approximate frequency of once in eight years during the last fifty years. However this frequency is regionally very variable, and some provinces, especially those in the mountainous regions of the west and the Gobi steppe and desert regions of the south, are more vulnerable than others.

Dzuud is a good example of covariate risk, to which poor households are especially vulnerable but which occur on a scale which makes it impossible for ordinary community or local support mechanisms to cope. Until the start of economic liberalisation, the Mongolian state carried the main share of such risks. Two mechanisms were especially important, in addition to the general support given by the *negdels* to affected households: a guarantee to supply supplementary fodder, and a system of livestock insurance. Although in theory these benefits were available only to collective animals, in practice they were also extended to private animals.

The emergency-fodder guarantee was extended through the State Emergency Fodder Fund (SEFF), which acted as the main channel between fodder farms and *negdels*. Established in 1971, the SEFF was originally intended to act as a supplier of last resort, moving fodder from the surplus areas in the central, northern and eastern *aimags* to deficit areas in the west and south. SEFF supplied fodder to *negdels* at cost at point of origin, with the state covering transport costs. As a result SEFF became a cheap source of fodder in deficit regions, and its original emergency purpose, although maintained, was diluted; the cost to the state of its operations became unsupportable, especially with the increase in transport costs accompanying liberalisation. Reforms started since 1990 have severely curtailed not only the fodder-marketing role recently undertaken by SEFF, but have also substantially reduced its ability to perform its emergency functions. SEFF now has only eight distribution points, and is unable to buy fodder because of cash flow shortages.

Livestock insurance was an original and successful feature of the Mongolian pastoral system. All *negdel* animals were insured, although different types of loss were treated in different ways. Losses from epizootic disease were considered to be a state responsibility, and were met by the state through the *negdel*. Losses from predation and accidents were considered to result from negligence, and were generally the responsibility of the herder. However, losses from natural calamities, especially *dzuud* and hailstorms, were fully covered by insurance; claims were subject to investigation by a permanent 'loss certification commission' in each *negdel*. Livestock insurance was successful in narrow financial terms, so much so that it was used to cross-subsidise crop insurance, where claims were often higher than premiums. However, insurance was seen as a *negdel* affair, and few private animals were insured. With massive privatisation of livestock from 1992, levels of animal insurance fell sharply, and are now very low.

Risk plays a key role in creating and maintaining poverty, and an anti-poverty strategy needs to include risk management. Issues include:

Emergency Policy. The government should develop a policy on rural emergencies, especially *dzuud*. This should set out the government's approach to emergencies, the actions to be undertaken both in advance of and during an emergency, and the resources available. Although *aimag* and *sum* governments should play a central role in the design and implementation of the policy, central government should retain final responsibility for coordination and resourcing such a policy.

Strengthening Customary Risk Management Strategies. The first response to individual risk occurs between kin and neighbouring households and within small groups. Policy should seek to strengthen such responses. Further work is needed to propose a detailed strategy in this area, but elements include:

- group insurance of private livestock, including perhaps those of individual *khot ail* camps, customary neighbourhood groupings, or more likely livestock companies; companies would negotiate an overall insurance plan for all their members' private livestock, the premium either to be shared among members or paid out of company marketing revenues; the company would provide a verification mechanism in case of claims; premiums would be graded according to the claims record of the particular company so that fraudulent claims would be discouraged; such insurance would be particularly important in the case of restocked animals, discussed above;
- creation of a *sum* poverty fund, available to groups such as *khot ails*, neighbourhood groupings or companies, which can demonstrate that assistance has already been provided to the household in question by the community; the *sum* fund would match community funds and assistance already provided;
- there is a need to investigate the potential of other customary quasi-redistributive mechanisms in herding society, including adoption, ceremonial feasts, urban-rural *idesh* exchanges, and fictitious 'brotherhood' relationships,[19] to serve as channels for formal sector support to poor individuals and households.

Strengthening Market Responses to Covariate Risk. There is a role for more sophisticated market responses to risk management, although these will need initial state assistance to demonstrate their potential. They include:

- further work to show whether the Mongolia-wide probability of certain risks, especially extreme winter conditions, permits an economically viable national livestock insurance scheme. The success of the previous *negdel* livestock insurance suggests that it would. If so, the state should take the initiative, with donor support, to create a parastatal insurance agency capable of handling livestock risks, with a view to turning it over to the private sector after an establishment period.

• development of fodder storage and marketing on a commercial basis in vulnerable areas, especially the western mountain and Gobi provinces.

Strengthening State Responses to Covariate Risk. An essential role remains, and will remain under foreseeable circumstances, for the state in managing covariate risk. The most important action is to reform the SEFF, with adequate resources, to perform its original role as a fodder supplier of last resort in emergencies. This would include providing adequate stored fodder at strategic locations to meet emergency needs, a transport capability (perhaps through the armed forces as before), and a procedure to declare local, provincial or national emergencies which is not eroded into an annual event. During the transition to new arrangements it is essential that support is provided by donors to SEFF to enable it to meet emergencies during that time.

INCREASING PRODUCTIVITY IN THE LIVESTOCK SECTOR

We have argued that the key problems to be resolved in rural development at this moment are institutional ones, arising particularly from the need to restructure the rural economy to allow it to function more effectively. Major investments in new technologies or rural capital will not be justified until the institutional framework is in place, and able to guide and provide the right incentives and disincentives to producers. This does not mean that no technical inputs can be useful. There are several technical issues to be resolved in the longer term, and a start should be made as soon as possible on design and testing under different local conditions. The three most important are grazing management and fodder, veterinary services, and technical training. Only the first of these is discussed in any detail.

(i) Grazing Management and Fodder

There has been some concern among Mongolian scientists and outside advisers about ecological degradation in Mongolian steppe areas, and about the possible aggravation of this by livestock sector interventions.

There are clearly areas, especially around towns and roads, where the pressure of grazing has been high. More generally, it seems likely that growth of the national herd has for many years been limited by a severe winter–spring pasture constraint. However, no detailed research has been carried out to demonstrate widespread environmental degradation. Indeed the small amount of research that has been reported, as well as similar work in other pastoral environments such as Australia and Africa, suggests that the dynamics of dry ecosystems such as much of Mongolia are more controlled by external factors, such as variable soil moisture availability, than by grazing intensity itself. Such non-equilibrial environments generally occur where the coefficient of interannual rainfall variation exceeds about 33 per cent, which in Mongolia corresponds to an annual rainfall total of around 265 mm or below; this covers the dry end of the typical steppe zone and all drier regions including the shortgrass steppe, desert steppe and desert, plus those mountain areas within desert zones where rainfall is below 265 mm, in total making up nearly half the country.[20]

More research is needed on these questions but, if confirmed, the findings suggest that large parts of the Mongolian pastoral environment exhibit the characteristics of an environment in which fluctuations in species-composition and productivity of pasture are more closely related to fluctuations in climate than to the density of grazing livestock. This view of ecological researchers is shared by herders, who generally do not believe there have been permanent changes in species composition or productivity of pastures other than in specific, generally peri-urban, places.

There is, on the other hand, no dispute about the importance of seasonal fodder deficits and the role of fodder production generally in the livestock economy. The Asian Development Bank's Livestock Feed Resources project proposal has developed ideas about specific technical options in this respect, including especially the development of ley or legume intercropping on abandoned arable land. These techniques need to be experimented on a small scale in specific local ecological and institutional situations. An *aimag* level project approach to rural poverty should include such testing of technical inputs.

(ii) Veterinary Services

The decline in state provision of veterinary services has potentially serious implications for livestock production. Indeed the survival rate of young animals has already declined from 96.2 per cent in 1989 to

87.2 per cent in 1993. The problem is how to maintain key veterinary coverage through the market and within the new organisational framework in the countryside. The European Development Fund veterinary service project has started work on this and should be associated with any project initiatives through the poverty programme.

(iii) Training

Mongolia has no rural extension service to diffuse new techniques or ideas, and limited rural training facilities, although the Agricultural University is making a start in this direction. There are several important issues related to extension and training, which are listed here without detailed discussion.

Mongolian herders have a long and extremely well-developed tradition of technical skill and innovation in animal husbandry. Although this tradition was to some extent undermined by the specialised techniques introduced during the collective period, the most important elements remain, as does a readiness to experiment and learn.

However, the rapid urbanisation of recent decades, followed since economic liberalisation by a reversed, urban-to-rural flow, has cut off many people from this tradition. This trend has been reinforced by the very young structure of the herding population, with many young households whose heads have recently left school with little technical herding knowledge. As a result, there are now many new herding households who do not master the traditional techniques, and they are likely to be among the poorest.

The first objective of training should be to capitalise on the existing pool of herder knowledge in order to bring the general level of skill closer to best existing local practice. Such herder-to-herder methods include using experienced herders as consultants between herder organisations, facilitating exchange visits between herder groups, and organising 'livestock shows', perhaps to coincide with *naadam* festivals, at which there would be competitions for the best animals, the most accomplished performers of particular animal-management tasks, competitions for the best cheeses and meat products, as well as demonstrations and trials of new techniques or machinery.

There is also, given low population density, a place for new approaches to distance learning and non-formal education, using radio and written extension texts. Project approaches to rural poverty should experiment with new extension and training methods of this sort.

NOTES

1. Government of Mongolia, *Mongolia: Policy Framework Paper*, 1993.
2. Paper prepared by the *ad hoc* Rural Working Group of the Government of Mongolia Poverty Alleviation Project, 1994.
3. The *bod* is a Mongolian horse unit: camel = 1.5 *bod*, cattle and horses = 1 *bod*, 7 sheep = 1 *bod*, 10 goats = 1 *bod*.
4. Institute of Development Studies, *Improved Livestock Feed Production, Management and Use in Mongolia: Socio-Economic Potentials and Constraints*, Asian Development Bank, Vol II: 119–24, 1993.
5. N. Uphoff, *Local Institutional Development* (West Hartford, Connecticut: Kumarian, 1986).
6. Robin Mearns, 'Pastoral Institutions, Land Tenure and Land Policy Reform in Post-Socialist Mongolia', PALD Research Report No. 3, Research Institute of Animal Husbandry (RIAH), Ulaanbaatar, and Institute of Development Studies (IDS), University of Sussex, 1993.
7. PALD, 'Options for the Reform of Pasture Land Tenure', PALD Policy Option Paper No. 1, RIAH and IDS, 1993.
8. Jerker Edstrom, 'Mongolian Pastoralism on Trek Towards the Market: Changes in the Production, Exchange and Consumption of Pastoral Products During Post-Communist Transition to a Market Economy', PALD Research Report No. 10, Institute of Agricultural Economics (IAE), Ulaanbaatar, and IDS, 1994; and PALD, 'Options for the Reform of Livestock Marketing in Mongolia', PALD Policy Option Paper No. 2, IAE and IDS, 1994.
9. State Statistical Office, *Statistical Yearbook*, 1994.
10. J. Edstrom, op. cit., 1994.
11. L. Cooper and G. Narangerel, 'Liberalisation of the Mongolian Pastoral Economy and its Impact within the Household – A Case Study of Arhangai and Dornogobi Provinces', PALD Research Report No. 8, RIAH and IAE, 1993.
12. J. Edstrom, op. cit., 1994.
13. Council of the Minister of Food and Agriculture, 'Basic Guidelines for the Development of the Food and Agriculture Sector', March 1993.
14. Although some researchers reject this hypothesis: see e.g. T. Potkanski, 'Decollectivisation of the Mongolian Pastoral Economy (1991–92): Some economic and social consequences', *Nomadic Peoples* 33: 123–35, 1994.
15. This section is based on G. Templer, *et al.*, 'The changing significance of risk in the Mongolian pastoral economy', *Nomadic Peoples*, 33: 105–22, 1994.
16. T. Potkanski, op. cit., 1994.
17. L. Cooper, forthcoming, *Nomadic Peoples*, 33, 1994.
18. B. Batbuyan, A. Enkhamgalan, Erdenebaatar, *et al.*, 'Natural and human factors in the management of Mongolian pastoral ecosystems under contemporary economic transition: An overview', Paper presented at the Conference on Grassland Ecosystems of the Mongolian Steppe, Racine, Wisconsin, 4–7 November 1993.
19. See T. Potkanski, op. cit., 1994.
20. Institute of Development Studies, op. cit., Vol 1: 9–10, 1993.

8 Crop Production and Small-Scale Rural Processing

Nadia Forni

Crops have always had a marginal position in Mongolian rural production because of the country's climatic and other natural conditions: the vegetation period is estimated at only 120–140 days per year in the south and 80–100 days in the north. The area classified as arable is estimated at 1.3 million ha, less than 1 per cent of the country's total land area. Only 50 per cent of this, or 657 000 ha, was actually cultivated in 1992, since the sudden increased cost of inputs, or their unavailability, made production uneconomic. The downward trend has been steady since 1989, when cultivated area accounted for 853 600 ha. The irrigated area reached 57 300 ha at the peak of its expansion, most of it under highly-mechanized sprinkler systems in 156 registered schemes now undergoing accelerated decay; there was also a limited area of 13 900 ha in unregistered schemes using low-cost surface-irrigation methods.

Commercial crop production did not begin until the 1960s with an emphasis on grains, predominantly wheat, which occupied 90 per cent of cultivated area in 1992. Fodder, potatoes and vegetables account for the rest. Vegetable production is entirely dependent on irrigation, while only 20 per cent of potato and 10 per cent of fodder production are irrigated. Irrigated cereal production has always been marginal.

The downward trend in production from 1989 has occurred in all these crops and can be explained both by the macroeconomic situation and organisational breakdown. The year 1989 represents in crop production, as for other sectors, the watershed between the past system and the liberalisation process still underway.

Unlike the livestock sector, with its many centuries of accumulated experience, crop production is a recent creation, mainly based on imported models and technology, and subsidised inputs. Because of the sudden disruption of the technological linkages with the former

Soviet Union, both in terms of supply and know-how, and of management difficulties in a changed market, the new production units must devise new structures without historical experience to assist them. Furthermore, while herders can retreat into a subsistence system to survive during the adjustment to a market economy, this is hardly possible in crop production units organised around single-crop specialisations. Workers' and employees' subsistence needs are mainly met from sources external to the firm. There is thus a distinct risk that the rural population employed in crop production will fall into deep poverty.

LIBERALISATION: SPLITTING FARMS INTO SMALLER UNITS

Crop production before liberalisation occurred mainly on state farms (73 in 1990 on the eve of liberalisation) and other large-scale state production units. By late 1992 these had been divided into more than 300 companies of different types.

Productivity in crop production had been low by international standards and it is expected that unavailability of fertilizers and other inputs at remunerative prices will cause a further decrease in yields. In the case of wheat, the main crop, grown in state farms following the Sovkhoz pattern in the wake of the Soviet Virgin Lands campaign, average yields were 1.2 tons per ha throughout the 1980s. Most inputs were obtained at preferential rates from the Soviet Union. After liberalisation such inputs have had to be bought with hard currency. Declining use of inputs and inability to replace and repair equipment is making wheat production steadily less viable economically, particularly in the more marginal areas. Some improvement seems however to be possible, particularly in the agriculturally better-endowed areas of the country, by increasing rotations with fodder crops.[1]

Under the liberalisation policies, the originally very large production units were to be privatised and transformed into smaller ones, organised as different types of companies. There was a very fast increase of such units in the early years of liberalisation, but the trend since then seems to have been reversed. Moreover the change from integrated state organisations to companies did not correspond to privatisation in most cases. In April 1994 there were 288 shareholding companies and these still accounted for most of the cropped area. There were 90 cooperatives (defined by assets not exceeding 500 000 tugriks), which covered about 30 000 ha, or an average size of 330 ha.

Individual farmers numbered 2000 and had a total of 60 000 ha, with a majority operating vegetable plots of about one half-hectare. Privatisation in the crop sector has been slower than in the livestock sector, in part because there are considerable doubts about its economic sustainability and in part because the debate on appropriate production structures is far from over. In this transition situation, many current production units are attached to research or other ministerial units. By early 1994, 51 per cent of all farms were still under state control.[2] In fact it is feared that, if privatised, many farms would quickly go out of operation and trigger a dramatic fall in the national food supply. In order to maintain production levels, instructions were given by government for cereal farms to be regrouped into units between 6000 and 10 000 ha in size, and the previous splitting into smaller units was reversed.[3]

THE EMPLOYMENT SITUATION

According to most observers, the crop sector suffers from surplus labour accompanied by seasonal shortages. State farm employees acquired 25 per cent of the shares of the units in which they were working in exchange for their privatisation vouchers. There are, however, insecurity about their continued employment and fears that many workers will join the ranks of the poor. In 1990 there were about 34 000 persons employed in the then state crop production sector, i.e. less than 3 per cent of the national labour force and 8 per cent of the rural labour force. In 1994 it is estimated that only half of that labour force is still employed.

Seasonal labour bottlenecks were in the past overcome by the use of labour gangs from the army or students mobilised at peak periods such as the harvest. The production system that eventually emerges after the transition is expected to absorb only a fraction of the labour force currently active in the sector, but there may still be considerable labour bottlenecks at peak periods. The organisation of exchange labour systems among different enterprises may have some beneficial effect but exchanges of labour are limited because of the coincidence of production peaks in summer in most rural activities. Recourse to some sort of mass mobilisation may therefore still be necessary.

POTENTIAL FOR EXPANSION

Economic analysis of current agricultural production units does not lead to much optimism. The sector was heavily subsidised under the centrally planned economy and its very existence could be justified only by food-security objectives. However, low yields are only partly due to obsolete or inappropriate technology, exacerbated by increased costs of inputs. A lack of comparative advantage, because of a poor natural resource base, is probably more important. Improved management through training and some technical upgrading are therefore unlikely to change the overall outlook fundamentally.

There may be scope, however, in specific cases to create value-added and employment. It is useful to focus attention on: (i) those crop-production activities that reinforce the productivity and sustainability of livestock production, which will continue as the mainstay of the economy; and (ii) production of perishable products such as fruit and vegetables or bulky products such as roots and tubers for urban markets, with high transport costs relative to their market value.

The case of fodder may merit particular attention because it is essential for livestock production. According to most observers, past production methods based on high-cost irrigation is not economically profitable.[4] However, side by side with increasing the area of cultivated pasture, technical findings have also suggested that expansion of specific types of fodder, particularly alfalfa, with limited fertilisation and irrigation, could be profitable.[5] This increased fodder production should be targeted on those *aimags* with some comparative advantage in terms of climate and access to water.

Another example is vegetable production, for which most technical experts conclude that there is a limited expansion potential because of lack of effective demand. According to some reports, a maximum planted area of 8000 ha would satisfy all potential demand. Investment in the vegetable sector, which has suffered from substantial equipment deterioration, should therefore be concentrated on only a limited part of the existing system.[6] A spontaneous growth of vegetable production is occurring in most peri-urban areas of the country and is, presumably, demand-driven. Furthermore, current prices are high for the average urban consumer and there may be considerable elasticity of demand if costs could be lowered, for instance by improving storage and distribution.

Moreover, spontaneous surface irrigation systems also are growing. Such schemes, only indirectly subsidised if at all, are characterised by low capital and high labour intensity and are likely to be organised by social groups with little access to assets or employment, such as female-headed households. They would therefore appear to be obvious targets in an anti-poverty programme.

CROP PRODUCTION AND POVERTY-REDUCTION

The crop production subsector is not expected to be a major component of a rural development strategy designed to reduce poverty in Mongolia. Nonetheless, it can play a small part. Some relevant aspects of an anti-poverty strategy are outlined below.

(i) Foodgrains and Fodder

The redirection of sectoral policies will affect access by urban and rural consumers alike to foodgrains. New policies may entail a reduction of the land area devoted to foodgrains, along with some increase in land productivity. An anti-poverty strategy in this area should therefore focus its attention on the poor mainly as consumers.

On the other hand, many farming units devoted in the past to foodgrains have the potential to be, at least in part, reconverted to fodder. The availability of fodder at affordable prices is essential for poor herders, who may otherwise be obliged to destock. Therefore, a poverty-conscious crop production policy will have to give priority to fodder schemes wherever these are technologically and economically viable. Each *aimag* should be assisted in establishing such fodder trials with technical support from the local agricultural offices and the national agricultural research institutions.

(ii) Crop Production as an Input into Household Subsistence

The increasing number of peri-urban, small town and *sum* level inhabitants involved in small-scale crop production, mainly potatoes, suggests the importance of 'urban' subsistence production in improving the diets of poor people. Self-provisioning has a role to play in containing the rise in the level of poverty. Self-provisioning should therefore be assisted. There are several ways to do this. For example, the organisation of seed distribution through the *aimag* and *sum* agricultural offices, at cost price, accompanied by simple leaflets on production methods, pest control and storage, should be most cost-effective.

Similarly, the scarcity of tools for simple agricultural work should not be underestimated. Credit for traders or artisans able to supply simple tools would be desirable.

(iii) Water Management and Irrigation

A better understanding of simple irrigation techniques could be promoted by technical assistance and training to groups of irrigators, particularly in the small non-registered irrigation schemes. This could be done through *aimag* and *sum* agricultural technicians. Group credit to buy pipes and other low-cost equipment should be included in the various credit programmes we have recommended.

(iv) Marketing

The development of private marketing channels for small-scale producers would enhance income generation. These producers may be supported by credit and business development assistance schemes.

RURAL SMALL-SCALE PROCESSING

Agricultural processing as a whole is an important sector in the Mongolian economy. It accounted in 1991 for 8 per cent of total employment and 40 per cent of industrial employment.[7] It is unlikely that its proportional importance has decreased since 1991, in spite of the overall drop in employment. In that same year the sector accounted for 52 per cent of manufacturing output, slightly over half from the non-food sector and the rest from the food sector.[8]

The reliance of agricultural industries on livestock production is evident. Livestock-based products dominate both in food processing, with dairy and meat products, and in the non-food sector, with hides and skins, furs, wool and the related carpet industry. The expected decrease in supplies caused by changed producer marketing strategies (discussed in Chapter 7) may affect this sector, at least in the short run, but the long-run potential remains high.

An important characteristic of the agricultural processing sector as a whole is its extreme concentration geographically, mainly in Ulaanbaatar, and an equally extreme concentration into large enterprises covering sometimes the entire national production. This pattern is only slowly changing as a result of liberalisation policies. For example, a large proportion of meat products in the country is still processed in the three large processing centres located in Ulaanbaatar, Darkhan and Choibalsan, working at 40 per cent of their capacity. Herders are reluctant to deliver livestock to these enterprises because of unattractive (monopsonistic) prices, and the firms' equipment is suffering from steady deterioration. Attempts to decentralise the process have not been successful.

With decreasing reliance on central procurement, and central planning in general, there seems to be scope for the development of agricultural industries which are more rural, in the sense of location and of their close connection with the agricultural production base. A spontaneous example of such a process is the development of small flour-mills, using cheap Chinese technology. Some 300 such mills were reported to exist in 1994, with some not operating because of inadequate repair and market changes following the import of cheap flour. The mills seem to have emerged, in a parasitic relationship with the state farms, to take advantage of the proximity of raw material supplies and the difficult access to supplies experienced by large flour-mills in distant locations. Most raw materials receive no local processing. Yet local processing could usefully occur either at the production level or in the *sum* or *aimag*, thus reserving costly transport for goods which have already undergone some processing and therefore have a higher ratio of value to weight. While this is in fact the declared policy of the government, the difficulties are formidable. Processing of hides and skins, as well as other valuable livestock products such as wool, are a case in point. The 13 factories that existed before liberalisation had become 20 or more in 1994, but they are operating at about half their pre-liberalisation production levels because of lack of procurement. Prices to primary producers are low, and procurement channels are in disarray.

Decentralisation of some primary processing within the *aimag*, desirable as it would be, requires careful planning. Wool washing, sorting and grading needs to be done under conditions which ensure quality, and the workers need to be trained. The economic size of local-level processing units needs to be determined, taking transport constraints into account. All these issues underline the need for a solid organisation at the *aimag* level. This can hardly be left to market mechanisms.

Also necessary is an improvement of local storage facilities. Traditional storage facilities seem to have suffered less from losses than modern structures based on capital-intensive imported models.[9] The spread and design of traditional storage methods should therefore be supported.

Local processing and storage activities such as these could have a substantial impact on women, as they are likely to engage a largely female labour force, even if only during the peak season. The high level of basic education of Mongolian rural women should make it possible for women to master the technology rapidly.

AGRICULTURAL PROCESSING AND POVERTY-REDUCTION

Successful promotion of small-scale processing will have a multiplier effect on the local and national economy and should therefore be a main element in a policy to eliminate poverty. To achieve this, timing and intersectoral linkages will be crucial. The strategy should reflect local circumstances and may therefore differ considerably from place to place. Hence we suggest that the *aimag* may be the best place to experiment with alternative types of organisation intended to promote rural development. Although details must be worked out industry by industry, some general principles can be outlined.

(i) Comparative Advantage

Small-scale processing will be most effective if it is based on local produce in relatively abundant supply. Therefore each major region and each *aimag* within it should identify its comparative advantage and develop activities accordingly. For instance, in areas where high-quality cashmere wool is produced, facilities for the primary handling of this product could be established, including transport and collection from neighbouring areas. Products of secondary importance in that area could be sent for processing to regions where that product is in more abundant supply.

Comparative advantage will have to take into account not only the availability of supplies but also market access and communications. An effective anti-poverty policy should be based on careful planning and feasibility studies, including the use of cost-benefit analysis for investment projects. Experience with local planning of this sort might best be gained in a pilot programme in one *aimag*. If additional resources were to become available, the experiment could be extended, say, to three contiguous *aimags* where possibilities for regional planning and a division of labour exist.

(ii) Scale of Production and Location

While processing activities may be conducted at the household, *bag*, *sum*, or *aimag* level, the most appropriate location of an activity will depend in part on inter-industry linkages and the minimum scale necessary to achieve profitability. There may well be cases where it is preferable to transport the raw material to the *aimag* centre for processing because of its location advantages, such as proximity to quality-control centres or superior infrastructure. In such cases the direct effect on poverty, in terms of employment creation, would be felt mainly in the *aimag* centre. However, the benefits would spread to the raw-materials producing areas through higher producer prices and a larger volume of sales, and hence additional income.

(iii) Management Support

To be effective in reducing poverty, small-scale processing will have to be competitive in national and even international markets, as in the cases of yak products and cashmere. Processing units will therefore have to be run as an efficient business, independently of their rural location. In order to help producers become efficient, they should have access to advice and training in production, management and marketing. Both training and advice can be channelled through federations of producers and professional associations, as well as provided by line ministries, e.g. the Ministry of Food and Agriculture for matters concerning raw material specifications and quality control.

(iv) Employment and Seasonality

The amount of employment generated directly by each unit is of course important. However, the most important consideration is the economic impact of the production unit, with all its backward and forward linkages, including its impact on employment and income through multiplier effects. Processing industries can have a great impact on poverty by absorbing seasonally unemployed labour. This is especially important in Mongolia because of the long periods of idleness during the winter, when most livestock activities and crop production come to a standstill. This implies that raw materials for processing in the off-season will have to be stored for perhaps several months, and hence investment in storage facilities may be required. There is thus a link between building and repair of storage systems and the economic efficiency of processing plants. Finally, small-scale processing, because of its disproportionate employment of female labour, is likely to be especially beneficial to poor women.

NOTES

1. N. A. Chalmers, *Wheat Production in Mongolia: An Economic Analysis*, PALD Research Report N. 7, RIAH/IDS/IAE, 1993.
2. Asian Development Bank, *Agriculture Sector Study of Mongolia*, 1994.
3. Ibid.
4. FAO and Asian Development Bank, *Mongolia – Irrigation Rehabilitation Project. Phase I*, 1993.
5. S. Jigjidsuren, *Policy Options for Improving Fodder Supply in the Transition to a Market Economy*, PALD, Working Paper N. 4, RIAH/IDS/IAE, 1993.
6. FAO and Asian Development Bank, op. cit.
7. Asian Development Bank, op. cit., 1994.
8. World Bank and United Nations Development Programme, *Mongolia: Medium Term Sectoral Priorities in the Transformation of the Economy*, Ulaanbaatar, 1993.
9. FAO and Asian Development Bank, *Mongolia – Agricultural Processing, Storage and Distribution Project: Phase I*, 1993.

9 Enhancing People's Participation

Seamus Cleary

Much recent discussion of the role of non-governmental organisations (NGOs) in development grew out of the increasing frustration of many donors at the apparent failure of existing delivery methods to benefit the poorest of the poor. In many cases, bilateral donors attributed this failure to venal and corrupt governments, more interested in increasing the wealth of their own client groups than improving the lot of the poor. The growing debate around questions of governance, public accountability, and democratisation focused increasing attention on NGOs and their claim of greater efficacy. They frequently asserted that the top-down project cycle was characteristic of the vast majority of development projects. By contrast, they claimed, their own approach was based upon a participatory partnership with the grassroots, empowering the latter with a sense of ownership. Much of this debate was further confused by lack of clarity over what an NGO was.[1]

Caught in the midst of this debate, which was often accompanied by declining levels of development assistance, many governments in developing countries became increasingly suspicious of NGOs and their activities, suspecting that donors were increasingly perceiving them to be alternatives to governments themselves. In the light of this, it is important to describe the broad outlines of an appropriate NGO role in a country's development.

NGOs are most frequently characterised by their reputed proximity to the grassroots. This has seen them effectively 'delivering services (inputs, seed, health education, etc.) or implementing projects such as road and canal building'.[2] Such practical grassroots actions have served to convince many in both development agencies and developing country governments that NGOs efficiently reach the poorest strata of a society while promoting poor people's participation in project design, implementation, and monitoring.

This is not to suggest, however, that NGOs are the answer to sustainable human development. Indeed, as Carroll points out, a number of myths surround grassroots organisations and community-based groups, in particular their capacity to organise and manage development. Furthermore, a number of additional constraining factors exist: the poorest people are often those least able to bear the costs of organising, thus working with existing groups alone may result in the poorest being bypassed. Nor, as Slater convincingly argues, are such groups necessarily as skilled at management, or as internally democratic as many would wish to believe.[3] As a result, it appears that more efficient access to the poor will result from a heterogeneous approach to enhancing the participation of the poor in their own development.

Experience suggests that NGOs have been most effective when working, either directly or indirectly, in partnership with government and other civil-society organisations. Such partnerships benefit from three complementary factors – political will, popular support and ownership, and cost-effective implementation. Where successfully sustained over time, advances in people's development will be achieved not least because of improved capacity 'to articulate the interests of citizens in institutions and local public agencies', thereby contributing to strengthened 'capacity building at local government level . . . an important requirement in Mongolia's new political environment'.[4]

MONGOLIA'S EMERGING NGOS

Prior to the initiation of the country's democratisation process, no Mongolian organisation was identifiable as an NGO. True, Mongolian peoples' organisations had existed for a considerable time but, given the overarching role of the state and party in Mongolian society, such organisations were adjuncts of either the state or the party, or both. In recent years, however, we have witnessed the withdrawal in 1991 of direct financing for a number of Mongolian peoples' organisations (such as the Mongolian Women's Federation, the Mongolian Veterans' Association,[5] the Mongolian Association for the Conservation of Nature and the Environment and the Mongolian Youth Federation) and the emergence of a growing number of new organisations. Among these latter are the Movement for Social Progress for Women, the Mongolian Association of Private Herders, the Mongolian Green Movement and the Central Council for Mongolian Children's Organisations. Lastly, Chapter 7 reports that a number of customary herders' institutions have re-emerged; among these the *khot ail* and the *neg nutgiinhan* are seen as potentially important for development purposes.

The federations which succeeded the earlier organisations began life with a number of significant advantages over the new organisations. Not least among these was a national network with many organisations having branches in each *aimag* and city. Among the most widely represented were branches of the Women s Federation (which also has members at *sum* level, frequently doctors working in the *sum* hospital), the Veterans' Association, and the Youth Federation. Trade unions are also widely represented.

A somewhat mixed blessing for the 'inheritor' organisations were the capital assets to which they also succeeded. While they were possessed of secure weatherproof premises in many instances, they also were faced with the task of identifying the resources required for their upkeep. The extent to which they have successfully achieved this while also assisting the poor and implementing training projects is a clear argument for believing that they have a long-term future.

The newer organisations which have been established face greater challenges. Many are run entirely by volunteers who are permanently employed in other jobs. This poses a substantial, but not insuperable, challenge to these organisations in their efforts to play a constructive role in the country's future development, not least because of the limited time which they are able to devote to their voluntary activities. More positively, their overheads are considerably lower than those of the 'inheritor' organisations, implying lower resource requirements in the short term at least.

It should not come as a surprise, therefore, that all of Mongolia's non-governmental organisations are still in the process of development. What is perhaps surprising is the extent and scope of many of their activities. For example, many 'inheritor' NGOs are already involved in efforts to respond to the growing socioeconomic crisis in Mongolia. Obvious examples include the Mongolian Red Cross, the Women's Federation, and the Veterans' Association. Activities which they have carried out include assisting *aimag* and *sum* authorities to identify the poor and provide assistance to the poorest and to provide training in health education and skills development.

Mongolian NGOs appear weakest at national level, lacking skills in administration, monitoring and evaluation of programmes which they undertake at *aimag* and city level. Additional expertise in these areas is necessary in order to increase their capacity to respond to the challenges confronting the country. The Mongolian Red Cross has sought to address this, with support from the German Red Cross initially, and subsequently from the International Committee of the Red Cross.

The Women's Federation has received more focused assistance; a UN volunteer oversees the administration of a UNIFEM project.

Mongolian NGOs suggest that the reasons for their weakness are twofold. On the one hand they are severely resource-constrained. The current legal position means that membership fees are the only means that Mongolia's NGOs have of developing an independent source of finance. The Mongolian Red Cross's experience underlines that although membership fees are a valuable means of institutional development, they can only make a minimal contribution to financial independence. NGOs in other countries usefully engage in productive activities, raising significant resources from, among other activities, trade. Were it legally possible for them to engage in productive activities such as marketing the goods produced by those undergoing skills training, Mongolian NGOs might usefully contribute to improving their difficult financial situation as well as increasing the supply of consumer goods on to the market.

Secondly, Mongolian NGOs emphasise their lack of information about each other's activities. This is understandable in view of the rapid emergence of the NGO sector in Mongolia and the constant increase in the number of NGOs. The importance of meeting and sharing information and ideas with each other has been recognised by the country's NGOs and this is to be welcomed and encouraged. Regular exchanges will contribute strongly to the further development and institutional strengthening of Mongolia's NGOs. It is desirable that the NGO community should determine the format for such exchanges themselves. UNDP staff and foreign NGOs have assisted in the development of information exchanges among Mongolian NGOs. This is to be welcomed and should be continued for the foreseeable future.

Despite this, one should not underestimate Mongolian NGOs' existing and potential contribution to the country's development. With good grassroots connections, a number actively assist local government both to identify and deliver assistance to poor families and persons, serving on both national and local committees established for this purpose. Furthermore, a number provide training to poor persons seeking to improve their prospects for an improved quality of life while others are active in public education programmes (for example, on environmental issues).

THE LEGAL CONTEXT

Government–NGO relations and cooperation in Mongolia are regulated at present by Article 19 of the Law on the Government of Mongolia, adopted on 18 May 1993. This broadly outlines the government responsibilities which NGOs may implement, as well as the duties of NGOs which carry out such activities.

Article 19 reads as follows:

> To impose some of the responsibilities of the government executive organisations upon other organisations:
>
> (i) The government imposes the particular duties of its executive organisations in the state coordination, information, analysis or research etc. or concrete duties of the substructure upon non-government agencies or similar organisations on the basis of the corresponding laws and government decisions and contracts and finances the expenditure related to their implementation.
>
> (ii) The organisation which takes over the particular duties of the government's executive organisations is directly responsible to the particular minister of the government of Mongolia and through him to the government of Mongolia for the implementation on the decisions of the government, especially if it is financed from the state budget.

Both the responsible Ministry and NGOs may propose projects for funding by the central budget; existing resource constraints have seen NGOs initiate the greater number of project proposals. Having identified the appropriate scope of NGO activity by mutual agreement between the NGO and the responsible ministry, the government makes available the necessary funding to the NGO. NGOs carrying out activities which are financed by budgeted project funds are accountable to the appropriate ministry for their activities on its behalf.

The government is in the early stages of drafting more comprehensive NGO legislation. At the time of writing, working groups to identify the components of this legislation had been established. An early draft of the proposed legislation defines an NGO as

> (i) ... an organised association of citizens with members and a charter voluntarily unified on the basis of common interests such as women's, veterans, disabled persons, children, youth, and student organisations, scientific, technical, ecological, cultural, sports, charity and hobby associations, professional, art, countrymen's unions and foundations.

(ii) Mongolian citizens are allowed to establish NGOs with the aim of protecting citizens' civil rights and freedom, to actively participate in public and state life, provide national professional needs, carry out charitable activities, educational, cultural, sports measures, preserve historical and cultural things, cultivate patriotic and humanitarian ideas, promote international relations and other activities not prohibited by Mongolia's legislation.

(iii) NGOs can be organised nationally, internationally and regionally.

NGOs whose purpose is to engage in propaganda which threatens Mongolia's independence and national solidarity, or with the intention of usurping state power, promoting violence, terror and mass disorder, discriminating against people on the grounds of nationality, language, race, age, gender, social status, wealth, employment, position, religion, ideology, education, or other activities creating fundamental human rights abuses, are prohibited. NGOs must submit an application for registration with supporting information comprising the name, aims, address, organisational structure, charter, programme, membership list, and financial information to the Ministry of Justice within 14 days of their establishment. The Ministry is required to complete the registration process within 21 days of the application's submission.

The draft proposes that NGOs should be self-financing. This position may be attained through NGOs operating their own businesses, levying membership fees, receiving donations from both Mongolian and foreign sources, and borrowing from foreign sources. The draft legislation also empowers the Ministry of Justice to request the courts to order an NGO to alter its activities or cease operations if there is proof that the NGO has violated the Mongolian Constitution, the legislation itself, or any other law [Article 11.iii].

An appropriate legal framework for NGOs is an important contribution to establishing the conditions for a participatory development approach. Hence the working groups should be encouraged to consult widely among the Mongolian NGO community concerning the framework and detail of the legislation. Without wishing to preempt any such consultation, we are of the opinion that a fundamental purpose of this legislation should be to encourage the further development of Mongolia's civil society and good governance.

Foreign NGOs working in Mongolia have a clear interest in the outcome of any such legislation, particularly as it affects them. At present, they are not required to register as foreigners with the Ministry of Population Policy and Labour if their activities are not conducted from commercial premises. But, if they open an office in commercial premises, the organisation's registration is necessary. This is done through the Ministry of Justice. (One foreign NGO, however, registered itself through the Ministry of Trade and Industry.) Information required commonly includes confirmation of sound financial status and confirmation that the person applying for registration is an official representative of the organisation. A registration fee of US $500 is also required. Foreign NGOs believe that this is excessive, particularly since they have been told that the fee for registration of a foreign commercial enterprise is US $10. Furthermore, many have found it necessary to employ legal representatives to undertake the registration process. This suggests that it is too complicated and underlines the urgency of enacting a legislative framework for NGO activity. Mongolian NGOs have emphasised their wish to contribute to the development of NGO legislation and their belief that its need is imminent.

We endorse the government's view that it has a responsibility to coordinate the scope of NGO (and other) activity in Mongolia while leaving the detail to individual negotiation. Thus the registration of domestic and foreign NGOs is both desirable and important. However, some of the registration requirements which must be met appear arbitrary and incompatible with the identity of an NGO. An example of this is the absence of legal identity for a non-profit organisation. The reputed difference in registration fees required from foreign NGOs and commercial organisations also appears arbitrary and unjustified. In the long run, such apparent arbitrariness and inappropriateness may prove a disincentive both to foreign NGOs and the Mongolian counterparts with whom they will work. This may well have arisen because of the relative lack of NGO experience within both the country and the government. To supplement local experience, other countries' legal frameworks and their experiences should be studied and adapted to Mongolia's circumstances.

GOVERNMENT–NGO RELATIONS IN MONGOLIA

Government responsibilities which NGOs may carry out include employment creation, training, research, poverty alleviation and social care. In practice, the responsible ministries notify potential NGO counterparts when project finance for particular purposes is available. On receiving this information, which is channelled through the local government structure, NGOs submit proposals for financing in the identified area.

It is planned that major project proposals will be considered at national level by a national-level council whose membership will comprise representatives of both government and civil society. This proposed National Council will replace the existing (and temporary) National Council for Poverty Alleviation which was established to assist in preparation of the government's poverty alleviation strategy, and membership of which includes representatives of the Mongolian Women's Federation, the Mongolian Youth Federation, the Veterans' Association, and the Mongolian Trades Union Federation. The government intends that membership of the planned National Council will increase the representation of civil society, not least through the inclusion of representatives of trades union and cooperative organisations. It is clearly important that any such National Council should be as representative of Mongolian civil society as possible. But in the interests of efficiency, it is also necessary to avoid a dysfunctional corporatism. It might be appropriate, therefore, for the civil society representatives on the National Council to be elected and their membership limited (e.g. to two terms maximum); they should also be representative of different interest groups in Mongolia (e.g. women, children, herders, workers, small-scale private-sector enterprises, veterans, etc.).

To date, government–NGO cooperation has been largely through the fairly well-established Mongolian NGOs. This is because the more recently established NGOs are believed to have little capacity to reach the grassroots. The government remains open to participation by new NGOs in its programme. It is seeking to strengthen the capacity of these organisations to reach the grassroots through support for training and participation in seminars. It is necessary that such institutional strengthening should continue and that as the ability of these organisations to implement projects effectively grows, those seeking to participate in appropriate programme identification, design, implementation, monitoring and evaluation as well as in the National Council be positively considered. Such an inclusive approach is an important means to overcome the risk of a self-perpetuating NGO monopoly which would be as counter-productive to participatory development as the total exclusion of all NGOs.

The government seeks to cooperate with all social actors in its efforts to overcome poverty in the country. Identification of those in poverty is carried out by local committees made up of the local administration's governor and social care worker together with at least three persons from the local community who are frequently representatives of NGOs in the area. The committee receives suggestions about potential beneficiaries of assistance from *horoo* or *bag* governors; this information is verified by visits to each potential beneficiary by the local administration's social care worker, who records detailed information relevant to family numbers, total income, and so on. Having verified the information, assistance is provided directly through local administrations (municipality, district, and *horoo* and *aimag*, *sum* and *bag*) and through NGOs.

THE MARKET ECONOMY AND CHANGES AT THE COMMUNITY LEVEL

The transition to a market economy has affected not only the economy but also civil society in general, and particularly the way people feel about their local community and the way local communities actually function. This is what one should expect since the change from central planning to a market-guided system does indeed constitute a systemic change. All aspects of society are affected, not just those which are primarily economic. The profound changes occurring at the community level were well expressed by a participant at a recent workshop on disadvantaged populations and the alleviation of poverty, who said, 'Before in the *sum* we had clubs, theatre, public baths, cinemas, newspapers. Now everything is closed because they are privatised and the owners don't run them.'[6]

These abrupt social changes within local communities can have serious effects on morale, dampening enthusiasm and even leading to depression and alienation. They can produce a sense of hopelessness and a feeling that individuals are powerless to help themselves. The market, far from being a liberating force, can appear to many, particularly those who fall into poverty, as an oppressive, soul-destroying and community-destroying force. Equally, people in remote *aimags* often feel cut off from national debates and national events, isolated and uninformed about what the transition means for them. Again, this was well expressed by another informant at the workshop who said, 'Gobi people have nothing . . . no information, no TV, no magazines, not even batteries for their radios.'[7]

The transfer of information as well as resources from the central to the provincial level is essential. Participation requires information, resources and a belief that one's own work can make a difference, even if only a small difference, in one's community. If these are lacking, participation, involvement and initiative will be dampened and the prospects for the poor will be diminished. The psychological effects of the transition on individuals and the social-psychological effects on communities should not be overlooked. There is more to poverty alleviation than economics.

CONCLUSIONS AND RECOMMENDATIONS

The practical value of civil society's day-to-day participation in poverty-alleviation programmes in Mongolia is openly acknowledged by both central and local government. Like the government, we believe that it is desirable and necessary to build upon this positive experience and expand it as additional resources become available. Hence we fully support the government's intention to establish a permanent National Council, some of whose membership will be from organisations representative of civil society. We also endorse the formalisation of the existing practical arrangements of the same nature at *aimag* and *sum* level. This represents a further step along the difficult road to the establishment of a fully-functioning civil society in Mongolia.

Thus far, such participation has taken place through what have been termed Mongolia's 'inheritor' NGOs. It appears that in many instances these NGOs are the most effective in reaching the grassroots. However, it is important for the further development of good governance and civil society in Mongolia that conditions do not emerge which permit the development of a monopoly NGO access to sources of governmental power and influence. Thus we recommend that access to NGO participation in the planned committees at national, *aimag* and *sum* levels be based on principles of efficiency, transparency and representativeness. Qualification for membership should include access to the grassroots, the client group, and accountability for the organisation's activities. Representativeness might be promoted by ensuring that membership of the committees reflects the area's different interest groups – women, children, herders, the unemployed, and so on. Democratisation might be usefully encouraged; local representatives of organisations representing different interest groups could meet to agree nominations to the committee. As a further safeguard against the possibility of one or another group of NGOs 'capturing' a committee in perpetuity, eligibility for membership should be restricted to a fixed period of time.

The role of the national, *aimag* and *sum* committees will be critical to the further advancement of participatory development in Mongolia. It is appropriate for the National Council to have two premier functions: first, it should develop with the Ministry of Population Policy and Labour for Cabinet approval the national guidelines for projects to be funded under the proposed emergency Growth, Employment and Poverty Alleviation Fund and assist in monitoring the application of these guidelines. Second, the Council will assist in the monitoring of the projects which are implemented and recommend the disbursement of the second and subsequent tranches of the Fund. *Aimag* and *sum* committees will identify the projects to be funded as well as who will implement them. Further, these committees will assist in monitoring and evaluating the projects, communicating information on them at regular intervals. In order to further encourage widespread popular participation, we also recommend that committee decisions should be taken on a consensual basis whenever possible. Where this proves impossible, it is desirable that a substantial majority of the committee express themselves in favour.

Poor herder families deserve particular attention. Re-emerged traditional forms of organisation, the *khot ail* and the *neg nutgiinhan*, may be particularly useful counterparts in this respect, both helping to identify those in poverty and, possibly, serving as communal guarantors for credit provided under the proposed emergency Growth, Employment and Poverty Alleviation Fund. We strongly recommend that the *sum* committees investigate the potential of these groups.

Despite the 'inheritor' NGOs' identified institutional weaknesses, their participation has had a beneficial impact on the lives of some of the people identified as being in poverty. Nonetheless, greater inroads into the eradication of people's poverty are attainable if the institutional capacity of Mongolia's NGOs is strengthened. This would not only enable central and local government to add to the pool of effective NGOs but also contribute significantly to the ongoing development of civil society. Institutional strengthening of both government (central and local) and NGOs is necessary in such areas as management capacity, project identification, monitoring and evaluation skills, and financial management. Part of this need will be met by the training component of the proposed technical assistance to the secretariat of the planned National Council. We also recommend that the UNDP mission in Ulaanbaatar set aside a small fund (US $100 000 annually for seven years) to be used for the institutional strengthening of Mongolian NGOs and local government counterparts. Activities should emphasise in-country practical short courses designed to strengthen

Mongolian NGO institutional capacity and improve their ability to maintain a creative response to the challenge of participatory development approaches.

Legislation covering the identity, purpose and activities of NGOs is inadequate at present; amendment to improve prospects for both domestic and foreign NGO activity is necessary. A constant area of concern confronting both Mongolia's 'inheritor' NGOs and their newer counterparts is resource scarcity. This has resulted in two unwelcome outcomes in the medium to long term. On the one hand, 'inheritor' NGOs have developed an unhealthy dependence on project finance for their survival. Experience of NGOs and civil-society organisations in other countries suggests that dependence on project finance weakens their performance capacity, not least because so much time is spent developing bankable projects. On the other, the country's newer NGOs face an equally daunting situation, operating as they do on a volunteer basis. This is not to question the valuable contribution to participatory development that volunteer organisations can make. But this contribution is necessarily restricted, not least because of the limited time available to volunteers to carry out such activities. It is concluded, therefore, that action to address such resource constraints is necessary.

It is illegal for Mongolian NGOs to engage in productive activities to increase their access to resources. A number of NGOs in other countries raise significant sums through their involvement in income-earning activities, including trade. Often among the items sold are goods produced by people benefiting from development projects which the NGO has financed or implemented. This appears particularly appropriate in Mongolia's context; consumer goods produced in the course of training programmes might be usefully sold. Not only would this contribute to increasing the supply of such goods in the (especially rural) market, but it would also contribute to the creation of demand from which the expected emerging micro-entrepreneurs can benefit. Profits accruing to NGOs engaging in such trade in other countries are also not taxed, provided they are used for charitable purposes. This ensures the greatest possible benefit to the NGO and its developing-country partners.

In a number of countries, NGOs are financed either wholly, or in part, by the government, fulfilling a number of important social tasks, including child care, assistance to the aged, advice to the general public, and financing development projects in and providing technical assistance to developing countries. Mongolia's tight budgetary circumstances do not permit this at present, even were it deemed desirable by both government and the community at large. In view of this, we urge the government to review legislation outlawing the involvement of Mongolian NGOs in productive activities and consider exempting from taxation the profits arising from such activities.

The number of foreign-based NGOs working in Mongolia has increased rapidly in recent years. The government is unaware of some of the activities and main purposes of such NGOs. This is both undesirable and inefficient as it often results in unnecessary duplication of effort and waste of resources. Thus the government's requirement that all foreign NGOs desirous of working in Mongolia should register with it is both understandable and desirable. However, many of the conditions necessary to meet the requirements of such registration appear arbitrary and inappropriate.

The government is in the process of drafting legislation with a view to regularising the situation. Legislation governing the activities of NGOs should be accorded priority and be enacted following the widest possible consultation with all of Mongolia's NGOs. In view of Mongolia's relative lack of experience of NGOs generally, a number of other countries' procedures and legislation should be studied and adapted to meet Mongolia's needs. Additional technical assistance in this area should be made available by the UNDP mission in Ulaanbaatar at the government's request.

NOTES

1. Clark and Cernea include grassroots groups, service organisations, and international non-governmental agencies in their categorisation of NGOs. Others are more selective; for these an NGO is an intermediary organisation which supports grassroots and popular organisations. For present purposes, the broader understanding of an NGO is preferred. (John Clark, *Democratising Development: The Role of Voluntary Organisations*, [London: Earthscan 1991] and Michael Cernea, *Nongovernmental Organisations and Local Development*, World Bank Discussion Paper No. 40, World Bank, 1988.)

2. Carroll (1992) cited in John Farrington *et al.*, *Reluctant Partners: Non-Governmental Organisations, the State, and Sustainable Agricultural Development* (London: Routledge, 1993).

3. Slater (1985) cited in *ibid*.

4. World Bank and United Nations Development Programme, *Mongolia: Structural Reform Agenda*, Meeting of Donors, Tokyo, 13–14 September 1993.

5. The Veterans' Association is an association of retired persons, not an association of ex-military personnel.
6. Report of a Workshop organised by the Ministry of Population Policy and Labour and the Save the Children Fund (UK) on 'Working With Disadvantaged Populations and the Alleviation of Poverty', Ulaanbaatar, 20–23 April 1994.
7. Ibid.

10 National Institutional Capacity for Addressing Poverty

Keith Griffin

The strategy for poverty-alleviation recommended in this volume has distinct implications for administrative organisation. First, within the strategy, responsibility for policy guidance, monitoring of progress and evaluation is assigned to the central government. Second, local government is given wide authority to select projects and programmes which address local conditions and then is held to be responsible for implementation. Third, participation by interest groups, non-governmental organisations and the community at large is encouraged both at the national policy level and at the level of local implementation. Let us consider each of these aspects of the strategy in turn.

CENTRAL GOVERNMENT ADMINISTRATION

In Chapter 2 it was stated that the dramatic rise in poverty that has accompanied the transition to a market-guided economy, and that has been such an unwelcome feature of it, caught the government by surprise. No specific policies to prevent the emergence of widespread poverty were included in the original set of economic reforms. No safety-net was created to catch those who might fall into severe poverty as a result, say, of rising unemployment, privatisation and restructuring or of the failure of money wages, salaries and pensions to keep up with price increases. No administrative structures were created, until recently, to address poverty issues. Policy issues were addressed as they arose; programme changes were improvised; a few small funds were created, the most important of which was the Social Assistance Fund; there was no coherent strategy to eliminate poverty and no institutional mechanism within the central government that was responsible for poverty as such. The Ministry of Finance and the Central

Bank were concerned about stabilisation; the line ministries (education, health, agriculture, labour) were concerned with their sectoral responsibilities; no ministry, board or council had a duty to safeguard the interests of the poor. Poverty fell through the cracks.

In 1993 it became evident that the incidence of poverty was high and rising, that a poverty-alleviation programme needed to be designed and implemented as a matter of urgency, and that a coordinating mechanism cutting across the conventional interests of line ministries needed to be devised. Thus was born the National Council for Poverty Alleviation.

The National Council is chaired by the Minister for Population Policy and Labour. It includes as members the Deputy Minister from four of the most important ministries, namely, finance, food and agriculture, health, and science and education. It also includes the Vice-Chairman of the National Development Board. Organisations of civil society participate on the National Council and at present there are members representing the Mongolian Trade Unions Federation, the Mongolian Women's Federation, the Mongolian Youth Federation and the Mongolian Veterans Association (which deals with the interests of retired persons and the elderly). Serving the National Council is a coordinating group and secretariat headed by the Director-General of the Population and Social Policy Department. The Council, in turn, reports to the Deputy Prime Minister.

The questions that need to be examined are the following: (i) whether the National Council provides the 'right' framework or umbrella for Mongolia's poverty-alleviation programme, (ii) whether the Ministry of Population Policy and Labour is the most appropriate to lead the poverty-alleviation effort and (iii) whether the Population and Social Policy Department has the capacity to coordinate programmes across ministries and act as the secretariat to the National Council. The answer to these questions is not obvious – and certainly not obvious to a foreigner unfamiliar with the nuances of Mongolian politics and the competence of every ministry and department in the public administration. Our advice therefore necessarily is based on a few rather general principles.

The first and most important principle is to work with existing administrative structures. These may need to be adapted to meet the goals of the poverty-alleviation strategy, and their capacity may need to be strengthened. The creation of separate structures in other countries has frequently proved to have negative effects on government capacity. Too often separate administrative arrangements have been made for high-priority programmes and experience suggests that this has usually been a mistake. *Ad hoc* arrangements have tended to become isolated from the established ministries, they have encountered resentment (especially if they benefit from special facilities, generous funding and off-scale salaries for the personnel involved) and they have often failed to elicit cooperation from other branches of government. In the specific case of Mongolia's poverty-alleviation programme, moreover, *ad hoc* arrangements are particularly unsuitable because anti-poverty programmes almost certainly will be needed for the indefinite future and hence the poverty-alleviation programme will require a permanent home and a permanent capacity within the administrative structure of the central government.

It is our view therefore that the existing National Council for Poverty Alleviation should be enhanced and restructured slightly, and the resulting new Council should be incorporated into the establishment and made permanent. It should report to the Prime Minister, since only the Prime Minister can take decisions which cut across ministerial boundaries and budgets. We think it right, too, given the severity of the poverty problem and the need for urgent action, that the Prime Minister should be directly involved. We recommend that the National Council be chaired by the Deputy Prime Minister. We further recommend, for reasons explained below, that the Vice-Chairman of the National Council be the Minister for Population Policy and Labour. The composition of the rest of the Council seems to be broadly appropriate at this time: additional ministries could be added from time to time as experience indicates that their activities have a significant impact on the level of poverty in the country. Herders and rural people generally are not well represented and one should add to the Council representatives from the National Council of Agricultural Cooperators and the Union of Production and Service Cooperatives. Similarly, other representatives from civil society organisations should be added if it appears that the voice of some sections of the poor is not being heard, or if new organisations arise which give effective voice to the poor. The composition of the Council, in other words, should not be fixed but instead varied in a pragmatic way as issues arise or disappear.

It is essential that the Council should have a broad mandate, covering macroeconomic, sectoral and regional issues. In particular, all future government strategies, policies, plans and macroeconomic programmes should be examined by the Council to see whether they address poverty issues explicitly. This is especially important because, as argued in Chapter 1, the emergence of widespread poverty in Mongolia has its origin in macroeconomic policy. The voice of the poor must be heard loud and clear when macroeconomic issues are on the table. The Council must not allow the discussion of poverty to be reduced to questions of social policy and income transfers.

The question of whether the Ministry of Population Policy and Labour would be the best lead agency is more difficult to answer. In most developing countries one would advise against assigning the lead-agency role to the Ministry of Labour because (a) it usually has little influence on economic policy as a whole, particularly macroeconomic policy, (b) it often is concerned primarily with wage-earning and salaried workers and largely ignores small farmers and herders and (c) its approach to poverty usually puts excessive emphasis on welfare payments, transfers, pensions and the social dimensions of poverty to the neglect of human capital formation and even employment-generation schemes. In Mongolia, however, the Ministry gradually is acquiring a broader vision and a deeper understanding of the poverty problem and of possible policy solutions. It might be an error to interrupt the learning process and change the lead agency now. In any case, no other line ministry would appear to be more suitable than the Ministry of Population Policy and Labour to play the leading role. The only alternative candidate would be the National Development Board, but so far at least, the Board seems not to have played a major role in thinking about poverty issues or devising suitable policies. On balance, therefore, we recommend that the Ministry continue to be the lead agency and that the Minister of Population Policy and Labour become the Vice-Chairman of the National Council.

The function of the central government, in partnership with the National Council, in the proposed poverty-alleviation strategy is to monitor progress in the reduction of poverty, to modify the strategy as necessary by correcting policies and introducing new ones, to allocate the available funds among the provinces, to monitor the implementation of programmes and projects at the local level, to evaluate the effectiveness of local activities and initiatives and to disseminate its findings among the population as a whole. Much of the burden of these tasks will fall to the secretariat. The existing secretariat, the Population and Social Policy Department of the Ministry of Population Policy and Labour, is too small and will have to be strengthened and enlarged.

Most staff members of the Department are either demographers concerned with population policy or analysts concerned with social policy. This group should be strengthened by the addition of two economists and a statistician who will focus on macroeconomic issues that affect poverty and questions of measurement at the national level. This team should be able to engage the Ministry of Finance, the Central Bank and the National Development Board in constructive dialogue and ensure that the interests of the poor are not overlooked. The Department also will need a small group, preferably of economists, to monitor and evaluate progress at the local level. Some training in microeconomics and in the elements of cost–benefit analysis would be useful. Frequent travel to the provinces and firsthand observation of programme implementation will be essential. Perhaps three such persons, responsible for six provinces each, would suffice. The United Nations Development Programme could be asked to provide financial support to supply United Nations Volunteers in order to launch this vital monitoring and evaluation service.

LOCAL GOVERNMENT AT THE *AIMAG* LEVEL

Under the proposed strategy, the governor of each of the 18 *aimags* or provinces would be directly responsible for designing the poverty-alleviation programme in his or her province, within guidelines established by the central government. The *aimag* administration also would be responsible for implementing its locally-designed programme both directly and through civil-society organizations and working with the *sum* (or district) administrations. (There are 325 *sums* distributed among the 18 *aimags*.) The province, in other words, would receive a budget allocation from the central government to be used to finance the provincial growth, employment and poverty-alleviation programme. Other resources mobilised locally would supplement the central budget allocation.

Implementation could be done directly by local government itself, or through existing non-governmental organisations, or through cooperative or communal institutions, or through institutions newly created for the purpose, or through local commercial banks. The choice would be made by the *aimag* government and no doubt would vary from one province to another. Most likely a combination of approaches would be used and this local experimentation should be welcomed by the central government, and indeed by external donors. In reaching a decision, however, the governor would be advised by a local council for poverty-alleviation on which all groups concerned with poverty programmes and the poor would be represented. As discussed in the previous chapter, participation by the poor and their representatives is essential to the success of the overall strategy.

The crucial assumption underlying the entire strategy being recommended is that local government has the managerial and technical capacity to design and implement anti-poverty programmes in partnership with local organisations in its area of jurisdiction. This assumption will be challenged by some, perhaps strongly challenged. One must admit straight away that the fiscal crisis of the state has reduced the capacity of government to manage any programme, including of course a poverty-alleviation programme. Low and falling real salaries have reduced morale in the civil service, led many to leave government to seek a livelihood in the private sector and made it difficult to recruit highly-qualified persons. Thus the participation of non-governmental organisations is not only desirable but may be a critical component for successful implementation. In practice, this is frequently recognised in Mongolia. This encourages our belief that the assumption of local competence is valid and we are confident in basing the strategy upon it. Indeed, compared to most other developing countries, Mongolia has a remarkably strong and effective structure of local government. This may be an inheritance from the years of central planning or it may be an imperative in a vast country (the fifth largest in Asia) with a small, scattered and isolated population (and one of the lowest population densities in the world). Whatever the explanation might be, the fact remains that local government institutions in Mongolia are well-developed and functioning efficiently. They are, however, starved of resources.

One of the features of the transition to a market economy in Mongolia is that the responsibilities of local government have been increased while budgetary allocations from the central government have been reduced. In the process the central government, after an heroic struggle, has barely managed to retain its fiscal integrity, but it has lost much of its programmatic substance. Local government, in contrast, has gained in terms of programmatic substance and freedom of action, but it has become as impoverished as many of the people it is trying to serve.

The central government not only has turned over responsibility for health and education expenditure to local government, it has given the *aimags* a lump sum budget and suggestions as to how it might be spent and then allowed each *aimag* to determine for itself how much should be allocated to health, to education, to the relief of poverty, etc. There is no financial mechanism at the centre to determine how much of its resources Mongolia will devote to human capital. Between 1990 and 1993, local government expenditure on education rose from

49 per cent of total educational expenditure to 90 per cent; between 1990 and 1992, local government expenditure on health rose from 78.8 per cent to 97.5 per cent of the total. During the same period the share of local government in total state revenues collapsed, falling from 53 per cent in 1989–90 to 17 per cent in 1993.

One of the results, as we saw in Chapters 4 and 5, is that total expenditure on human capital fell very sharply: in the case of health from 5.4 per cent of gross domestic product in 1990 to 2.0 per cent in 1993 and, in the case of education, from 11.3 to 3.1 per cent over the same period. In addition to human capital, local government is being forced to assume more responsibility for physical capital formation, employment creation and the alleviation of poverty through direct transfers to individuals and households.

There is no doubt in our mind that local government as an institution has the capacity to design and implement poverty-alleviation programmes, but it cannot possibly discharge its new responsibilities without a substantial injection of resources. There is a 'moral economy' in rural areas, i.e. a tradition of mutual assistance and solidarity in times of need, but the moral economy is weak, limited and in grave danger of being overwhelmed by the scale of the poverty problem it confronts.[1] Local government is the only institutional structure strong enough to make a real difference to the prospects of the poor.[2]

Assuming an injection of resources is in fact forthcoming, one must anticipate that mistakes will be made, that not all projects and programmes will succeed and that some provinces will do better than others. Local government has no experience in managing budgets of the size required to make a significant impact on poverty. It will learn by doing – and by observing the experiments of others. Lack of experience, however, is not synonymous with lack of competence and we believe that, if given the resources, local government can do the job. Indeed local government probably is the only institution in Mongolia capable of doing the job.

OTHER LOCAL INSTITUTIONS

Having said this, it is also true that other local institutions have a contribution to make and should be involved with the poverty-alleviation programme. In general, local institutions are weak, lack funds and require nurturing. Often, however, they are well-informed and can be articulate defenders of the groups they represent. They are a source of advice and in some cases they may be able under local government leadership actually to design and implement components of the local poverty-alleviation programme.

The range of institutions operating at the local level is considerable. Groups representing women, young people and the elderly – some well-established, others new – exist in most localities. The trade union movement often is well represented. The Mongolian Red Cross has an extensive network of branches throughout the country, but as is true of many non-governmental organisations, the branches are struggling to survive. Indeed many NGOs are born, flourish briefly and die: the problem for local government will be to decide which organisations have a viable future and are worth supporting and which should be left on their own to sink or swim.

A number of local institutions exist to encourage production or facilitate marketing. Formal small cooperatives can be found and their activities extended slightly to cover other purposes. In other cases, new cooperatives can be encouraged as part of an employment creation and investment programme. In still other cases informal cooperative or communal institutions exist, are being formed or are re-emerging after the dissolution of the *negdels*. A prime example in some regions is the gradual reappearance of the *khot ail* among herders, a mutual support group that existed prior to collectivisation. Cooperative and communal institutions clearly deserve support: they have emerged spontaneously to help people cope with pressing needs, they contribute to efficient resource management and increased production, and in an important although modest way, they form part of an informal social safety-net.

The non-governmental local institutions are often frail reeds from which to construct a poverty-alleviation programme, but at the very least, government should not obstruct their development and in the best of circumstances, these local institutions of civil society can join local government as partners in promoting development and reducing poverty.

NOTES

1. The moral economy is weak in Mongolia partly for historical reasons, namely, the long dependence for assistance on large institutions, the Buddhist monasteries in the pre-revolution period and the state since.

2. A UNDP-financed Management Development Programme is currently underway. One purpose of this programme is to strengthen the capacity of local administrations and better equip them to operate within the newly-decentralised structure of governance.

11 The Possible Contribution of External Agents

Keith Griffin

Future development in Mongolia, as in other developing countries, will depend primarily on national efforts. External agents can contribute to accelerated development in various ways, but their contribution will undoubtedly be modest. It is better to formulate policy on the assumption of self-reliance, and then be pleasantly surprised if international assistance is received, than to plan on a large inflow of foreign aid, and then be disappointed when the aid fails to materialise in the volume and form anticipated. Moreover, if development policy as a whole is well-formulated, the effectiveness of whatever amount of aid is received is bound to be greater than would otherwise be the case. The exceptionally large amount of aid received by Mongolia in recent years in comparison with its gross national product is likely to be temporary, a reflection of foreign interest in the country during its transition to a market economy. If the past is an accurate guide to the future, the attention of foreign donors can be expected to shift to other countries and other priorities in response to changes in the world economy as well as changes in economic and political conditions in the donor countries themselves.

Provided the management of the transition from here onwards improves[1] and provided the poverty emergency can be contained and measures introduced to increase the well-being of the poor,[2] there are reasons to be optimistic about Mongolia's prospects. First, the stock of human capital in Mongolia is exceptionally large compared to other developing countries with a similar standard of living. The population is well-educated and trained, it is well-nourished and enjoys good health. True, the education system is in crisis and there is a grave danger – indeed a virtual certainty – that the children of today will be less-well educated than their parents.[3] It is also true that the transition has not been good for the health of the people.[4] Morbidity and mental distress have risen dramatically; the maternal mortality rate has increased; the birth rate has fallen precipitously in response to the sharp decline in average living standards and to the rise in poverty. Even social health, as reflected in an increase in crime, has deteriorated.

The stock of human capital is deteriorating and the decline must be reversed as a matter of urgency. Expenditure on human capital is an investment in a country's people. It is, moreover, an investment with a high rate of return, indeed a rate of return that compares favourably with returns on investment in physical and natural capital. Expenditure on human capital is also a good way to ameliorate poverty in the short term, particularly what we have called 'capability poverty'. Thus on grounds of accelerating growth and alleviating poverty, there is a strong case for giving priority to human capital formation. Mongolia must not throw away through neglect the comparative advantage it now has in its stock of human capital.

Second, Mongolia's geographical location is a great asset that must be properly exploited. It is adjacent to one of the largest and fastest growing economies in the world, namely, China. It is within a short distance of an economy with a huge surplus of savings available for investment abroad and which is a major source of advanced technology, namely, Japan. Mongolia also is close to South Korea and within striking distance of the whole of East Asia, by far the most dynamic part of the world economy. Finally, Mongolia also is adjacent to Russia, another large economy with which she has close historical ties and which, sooner or later, is bound to recover from its own transition crisis and begin to grow again. When that happens, Mongolia literally will be surrounded by countries with enormous and rapidly growing markets, by countries with sources of savings looking for profitable outlets and by countries which can supply some of the best and cheapest technology in the world. All Mongolia need do is integrate its own economy closely into the economy of the region of which it is a part.

This implies, of course, that Mongolia should create an open economy based on its comparative advantage in human capital, minerals and livestock products. The set of incentives – price incentives, tax and subsidy incentives, regulatory incentives – must be carefully designed to encourage the employment of labour, reduce unemployment and increase output valued at world market prices.[5] Although in some sense Mongolia in normal times could be considered a labour scarce economy,[6] there is clearly surplus labour at present in the form of large numbers of women and men who either are unemployed or have only part-time employment. This surplus labour should be treated as an asset and mobilised for productive purposes, ideally on capital construction projects.

Similarly, Mongolia must make certain that relative prices, regulations and international trade policies in general encourage a shift of resources and a rise in investment in those economic activities in which the country enjoys a comparative advantage, or in which a comparative advantage can be created rapidly. A good example of what not to do is the prohibition of exports of cashmere. This is self-inflicted injury which is simultaneously foolish, inequitable and poverty-augmenting. The export ban, which led to an immediate fall of 40–50 per cent in the domestic price of cashmere, is foolish because it lowers supply, encourages smuggling, increases inefficiency and reduces average incomes in a country where incomes have fallen sharply; it is inequitable because it increases inequality in the distribution of income, which in any case has become much more unequal since 1989; and it augments poverty because cashmere is a product produced by relatively poor people and is a major source of income for many of the poor. There is a lively export market that should be exploited to the full. If the domestic cashmere industry cannot operate profitably, it should be closed down and not subsidised by turning the internal terms of trade against nomadic herders.[7] It would be a mistake for any small country to turn its back on profitable trading opportunities, but for Mongolia to do so in present circumstances borders on madness. Mongolia, to repeat, has a rare opportunity to integrate its economy into the most dynamic regional economy in the world. It must not throw away that opportunity.

The third reason for potential optimism about Mongolia's prospects is paradoxical: so many things have been poorly managed that there is scope for enormous improvements that could raise incomes of the poor (and others) quite considerably. If the transition had been handled perfectly and still incomes were falling, there would be cause for despair, but precisely because the economy is so inefficient, saving rates are so low and the investment pattern is so irrational, a serious attempt to correct mistakes could lead to spectacular improvements in the well-being of the population. Let us consider a few examples.

The commercial banking system is in chaos. There is an excess of credit creation (which results in rapid inflation and changes in relative prices that are hard to interpret) combined with government-directed credit allocations (which lower the efficiency of investment and the rate of growth). At the same time many of the potentially most productive sectors of the economy are deprived of credit: small business in general, the export sector, agriculture and livestock, and all of the economy that lies outside the major urban centres. A reallocation of credit (at positive real rates of interest) to where it could be used most productively would increase efficiency, raise incomes, accelerate growth and reduce poverty.

We have already mentioned the malfunctioning of the labour market and the neglect of human capital formation. Opportunities to mobilise labour for productive investment in public works and other activities are being wasted. If idle human resources were put to work, output and incomes would increase, growth would be encouraged and poverty would decline. A similar point has also been made about wasted opportunities in international trade. It is remarkable that traders in general, but particularly those engaged in international trade, are looked down upon not only by the public at large but also by many senior government officials. Yet the future of Mongolia depends on trade and traders. Comfortable isolation is not an option; the alternative to trade is continued poverty.

And lastly, there is the agricultural sector.[8] The livestock economy is the backbone of the country, yet it has been treated so negatively that were it not populated by tough, resilient and resourceful Mongols, it would have entered into terminal decline some years ago. It has been starved of investment, and as a result, the lack of transport infrastructure makes marketing difficult and costly, and the lack of power makes local processing on a commercial scale virtually impossible. The small size of the market makes specialisation and division of labour virtually impossible to achieve. The *aimag* economies are largely self-contained, suffering from high 'natural' protection resulting from very high transport costs. There is a need at the regional level to invest in transport and power infrastructure in order to create more integrated local and regional economies and permit a greater division of labour. After the dissolution of the *negdels*, even specialisation at the household level became more difficult and diseconomies of small scale emerged, reflected in an increased demand for household labour. In effect the herders have become trapped in a self-provisioning subsistence economy.[9] To make matters worse, policies during the transition have turned the terms of trade against the livestock sector and government regulations, as we have seen in the case of cashmere, have created obstacles to export. As a result, there has been a retreat into barter, a withholding of supplies from the domestic market and a resort to smuggling. The collectives (*negdels*) were dissolved, the herds were privatised precipitously and land rights and land management were left in a state of limbo. Finally, to add insult to injury, the neglect of the livestock sector is justified in some circles by the claim that herders are relatively well-off and are not poor.

The fact is that most herders are not well-off and many are poor. The livestock sector, however, has considerable potential and could be the leading sector in a recovery of growth. If its institutional arrangements were stabilised, if it were allowed to export freely, if its terms of trade were improved, if even a modest amount of investment were allocated to the rural areas, and if the banking system could organise itself to provide finance capital on the basis of herders' assets in animals, the rural economy in general, building on expansion in the livestock sector, could experience a rapid rise in incomes, output, savings and growth, and a significant decline in poverty.

These examples illustrate what is possible. Mongolia potentially could experience sustained economic growth and its population a substantial increase in well-being. None of the measures suggested requires a large injection of foreign capital, a massive transfer of technology or large numbers of foreign advisers, consultants and experts. Mongolia could quickly become self-reliant if it were prepared to change its priorities by favouring investment over consumption, employment over capital intensity, an open over a protected economy and rural over urban development. If these shifts in emphasis were to occur, foreign assistance would no longer be needed, although it should continue to be welcome, since its contribution to Mongolia's development undoubtedly would be greater in the context of a well-functioning economy than it is now.

PRIVATE FOREIGN CAPITAL

There are two conditions that must be satisfied in order for a developing country to attract private foreign capital in significant volume. First, there must be an adequate infrastructure, at least in the largest city and preferably throughout the country. Power, transport and communications are the foundation of a modern economy and if these are lacking or are unreliable, foreign investors are likely to go elsewhere. If the central city is populous and well-provided with infrastructure, some foreign capital may be attracted to serve the urban market or produce for export, but unless basic infrastructure exists throughout all or most of the country, and creates an integrated national economy, foreign investment will be unable to operate on a national scale to produce import-competing goods or export products based on processed raw materials drawn from several regions of the country. This is especially true in small economies like Mongolia.

Second, foreign capital is attracted to growing economies, not stagnant or declining ones. Private foreign investors are attracted by profit opportunities, not obvious 'needs' or by 'scarcity' of capital. Unless growth is occurring, and can be expected to continue on a sustained basis, foreign investors are unlikely to perceive profit opportunities and private investment is therefore unlikely to be quantitatively significant. Notice that it is the expansion of the national economy that creates profit opportunities which, in turn, induce an inflow of private capital. That is, the direction of causality is from national growth to foreign capital, not the other way round. It would be a mistake to imagine that foreign capital can be the catalyst, let alone the major ingredient, and growth of the national economy the result. Those who wait for foreign investment to initiate growth are likely to wait indefinitely.

The exception to these two generalisations is countries which are endowed with a large quantity of a valuable natural resource. Where there is an abundance of oil (as in Saudi Arabia) or of diamonds (as in Botswana), foreign capital can be attracted in large volume to exploit the natural resource for export. Unfortunately, however, Mongolia is not one of the exceptions. Although it has exploitable mineral deposits, these are not available in sufficient quantity or quality to attract a large inflow of capital. It is possible that in future valuable deposits of mineral ores, petroleum or gas will be discovered, but for the time being, massive private foreign investment in the mining sector can be ruled out.

This brings us back to the two preconditions for private foreign investment: adequate infrastructure and sustained growth. Alas, Mongolia fails on both counts. The infrastructure is unusually poor and the per capita rates of growth of output and income have been negative for several years. One is forced to conclude, therefore, that Mongolia cannot expect to be a recipient of a large inflow from abroad of private capital. Nonetheless, Mongolia should be receptive to foreign capital: it should place no obstacles on foreign investment nor should it subsidise it in any way.

It is possible that Mongolia may be able to attract small amounts of foreign investment in a variety of activities. Minerals, tourism and the processing of livestock products (wool, camelhair, leather, cashmere) are obvious possibilities. Small-scale foreign investment in Ulaanbaatar also is possible, for example, in restaurants, hotels, urban transport, retail shops and wholesale facilities. All such opportunities to attract foreign capital should be grasped, regardless of the national origin of the investor and the sector of economic activity. Mongolia desperately needs the jobs, income and growth of production that foreign capital can provide, even if it is bound to be on a modest scale.

OFFICIAL FOREIGN AID AND TECHNICAL ASSISTANCE

No country has become developed by relying heavily on foreign aid for a lengthy period of time. All the countries that once were underdeveloped and are now considered to be developed achieved their success through their own efforts. There are no exceptions, not even Mongolia, which received massive foreign assistance from the Soviet bloc for four decades. This sober historical fact underlines the importance of national resource mobilisation, national development-oriented institutions, high national savings rates and national human capital formation. Foreign capital in the form of grants and loans on concessional terms can in principle contribute to the development process, but it cannot be a substitute for domestic initiative and effort. Sooner or later Mongolia will have to adjust its policies so that it becomes much less dependent on foreign assistance and the sooner this occurs, the better for the people of Mongolia.

Soviet aid was replaced by aid from a multiplicity of sources beginning in 1991. As indicated in Chapter 1, Western aid did not fully compensate for the loss of Soviet aid, but it did cushion the blow and should have made it possible to begin the transition to a market economy without excessive disruption from external shocks. It probably was and is the case, however, that Western aid is less convenient or useful in some respects than was Soviet-bloc aid. First, the multiplicity of sources can generate confusion, delay, conflicting criteria and procedures, duplication and waste. There are 24 bilateral donors in Mongolia (of which Japan is by far the largest) and more than 14 multilateral donors, including non-governmental organisations (of which the Asian Development Bank is by far the largest).

Secondly, most of the aid is tied in one way or another and much aid is tied in more than one way, namely, to source of procurement, to a particular project or programme, to the foreign exchange component of a project or programme, to the adoption of particular policies, and so on. Donors spend much time discussing the need for aid coordination – it is a perennial and favourite indoor sport in aid agencies – but in practice the donors largely go their separate ways, grinding their bilateral and multilateral axes and shaking their heads over an alleged inability of the recipient country to use aid efficiently. The myriad knots tied by a host of donors is mysteriously transformed into a lack of capacity on the part of the recipient, as if the lack of capacity suddenly emerged the day after the Soviet aid programme ended.

Thirdly, each donor, quite properly, is concerned to ensure that its aid is used as intended, that costs are kept to a minimum, that corrupt practices are avoided, etc. The result is a multiplicity of monitoring, reporting, review and auditing arrangements, each imposing a burden on the recipient country. The aid 'process' involves frequent travel – and very high overhead costs – to 'find facts', assess the country's economy, establish an 'operational framework' for the donor's aid, to conduct pre-project investigations, to appraise the project, monitor progress and, finally, to conduct a *post mortem* examination. All of this 'technical assistance', supervision and evaluation absorbs an inordinate amount of time of senior government officials. Indeed many officials spend more time servicing foreign missions than serving their people. In extreme cases officials come to believe that the two are indistinguishable.

Mongolia also has been the recipient of genuine technical assistance. The most valuable assistance is provided by those who reside in Mongolia for an extended period or who visit the country frequently over a number of years for several weeks at a time. There are relatively few such people. Most technical assistance is provided by 'experts' who do not know the country and who stay for only a short period – a few days, perhaps several weeks, occasionally for one or two months. The assistance provided is a report, of which this study is an example, containing analysis, advice, recommendations, suggestions for projects and programmes and, often, the observation that more technical assistance is required.[10]

Probably no one has counted the number of 'missions' that have visited Mongolia since 1989 or the number of reports that have been filed, but there must have been hundreds of missions and scores of reports. Mongolia, indeed, suddenly has become a much-studied country and possibly the most studied of any country of its population size. Many of these studies undoubtedly are valuable and much free advice has been offered, but one is struck by the blandness of many of the reports, of the rather conventional and unimaginative views expressed. Above all, on the really vital issues (macroeconomic stabilisation, price liberalisation, privatisation, property rights in land, employment creation, economic growth) one is struck by the absence of a second opinion from an opposing perspective. The 'expert', whoever it may be, is assumed to have a monopoly of wisdom in the area of his expertise. This of course is nonsense, and just as one would not undergo a heart-transplant operation without seeking the advice of at least two surgeons, a country ought not to embark on a change of economic regime without seeking a variety of views on how best to effect the transition. The value of technical assistance would increase quite considerably if more of it consisted of second opinions on strategic issues.

More second opinions on strategic issues would have the great advantage of giving Mongolia greater control over the aid process and over its own destiny. Whether the amount of aid received is large or small, the government must remain in control, must be in a position to impose conditions on its side, and must be able from time to time to say 'no' to a donor. Only the Mongolian government is in a position, after all, to judge whether foreign assistance really assists. The preparation by the government of a poverty-alleviation programme gives Mongolia an opportunity to design a coherent approach to the problem, to identify areas where foreign donors can contribute effectively to nationally determined priorities, and to prevent aid agencies from pursuing their own agenda and undermining the government's priorities by introducing a patchwork of initiatives which often create more difficulties than they solve.

NON-GOVERNMENTAL ORGANISATIONS

It is in the area of second opinions where non-governmental organisations (NGOs) have a vital role to play. Foreign NGOs come in many forms: some are advocacy groups, often promoting unconventional views and approaches outside the mainstream of conventional thought; some are active in local, small-scale development work, often among the poor and occasionally experimenting with 'alternative' development approaches; some are engaged primarily in temporary relief activities, almost always among the poor; some focus on specific groups of the population (women, children, the handicapped), groups that in Mongolia sometimes are classified as 'vulnerable'. NGOs such as those described – and not all NGOs are relevant to a poverty-eradication programme – can be extraordinarily useful.

They are in touch with the grassroots and can be unusually well-informed. They can convey a worm's-eye view of problems to those in distant capitals. They can be a source of information about what works and what does not work at the local level. They can implement 'pilot' projects, undertake small-scale experiments, attempt to 'empower' local people, raise 'consciousness'. They can also be a great nuisance, proselytising alien religious doctrines and undermining local culture, mindlessly promoting views that would be totally unacceptable in their own countries, interfering in the political process in an irresponsible way. NGOs, in other words, are like all other human institutions: they can be a force for good or for its opposite.

What foreign NGOs rarely do, however, is supply capital on a large scale and on a sustained basis, unless in effect they are transformed into an implementing agent of an external donor, in which case they cease to be an NGO. Nor can they provide large amounts of technology or technical assistance. The scale of operations of NGOs, separately or collectively, usually does not permit them to have a macroeconomic impact. Their contribution, as far as development and poverty-eradication are concerned, is at the micro-level – and at the level of ideas.

In the end, of course, it is ideas that change the world, not capital, not technology and certainly not foreign assistance. Ideas, to be sure, must be translated into action by people with clear objectives and the determination to achieve them. NGOs can supply some of the ideas, but the objectives, the determination, the effort must be supplied by the country itself. The eradication of poverty in Mongolia is an idea whose time may have come and, if so, external agents can help to realise that idea in a variety of ways, but the commitment to the idea and the energy necessary to see it through to a triumphant conclusion must come from the people of Mongolia and their government.

NOTES

1. See Chapter 1 for a discussion of macroeconomic policies.
2. See Chapter 2 for an analysis of the extent of poverty and a suggestion for an emergency poverty-alleviation programme.
3. See Chapter 4 for a discussion of the educational system.
4. See Chapter 5 on health, nutrition and population policy.
5. See Chapter 3.
6. Labour is scarce relative to grazing land; it is abundant relative to physical capital.
7. If, after careful economic analysis, a convincing case can be made on infant industry grounds for government support of the domestic cashmere industry, that support should be provided not by a prohibition of exports of cashmere but in a transparent way by direct cash subsidies

from the government to enable industrialists to purchase cashmere on the open market at world prices. Such a subsidy presumably would require either an increase in taxation (e.g. a higher sales tax) or a reduction in public expenditure in other areas thought to be of lower priority (e.g. lower spending on urban hospitals).

8. See Chapters 7 and 8.
9. According on the Ministry of Agriculture, 66 per cent of herders' expenditure is on food, of which 78 per cent is self-provisioned; 54 per cent of all expenditure is self-provisioned.
10. For a critical evaluation of technical assistance, see the 1994 report of the United Nations Committee for Development Planning.

Index